250 Things
a Landscape Architect
Should Know

The publication was made
possible by the kind support of:

GreenBlue Urban Ltd

Marshalls plc

Vestre Ltd

250 Things
a Landscape Architect
Should Know

B. Cannon Ivers (ed.)

Birkhäuser
Basel

Foreword

Ed Wall, July 2021

Michael Sorkin was a master of lists. From *Local Code* to "Eleven Tasks for Urban Design" and from "A Merry Manifesto" to "The Sidewalks of New York", Michael employed lists as he crafted manifestos, design codes and urban agendas. While they rarely repeat, they all articulate common concerns – even when revealing tensions and contradictions. As with "Two Hundred Fifty Things an Architect Should Know", the inspiration for this book, brilliantly edited by Cannon Ivers, Michael's lists consistently express his desire for walking, his faith in cities and his confidence in the future.

Almost 20 years ago I was a student of Michael's, and ever since I have been immersed in his world of "Two Hundred Fifty Things…": studying urban design, living in a Manhattan walk-up, enrolled in a public college, learning from his designs, listening to his friends, encouraged to draw, supported in research. From fieldwork in Soweto to seminars with Jane Jacobs, and from readings with Marshall Berman to designing "exquisite corpses", the world that Michael generously shared was a constellation of the lists he wrote. During this time, he only once recommended we read one of his books. Frustrated with the urban codes that he had asked us to compose, he requested we read *Local Code: The Constitution of a City at 42° N Latitude*. I dutifully visited Labyrinth Books on West 112th and Broadway, read it in the store, bought it and have reread it many times since.

The urban code that I subsequently wrote was the basis of a proposal for the industrial district of Willets Point, Queens. It began with: "Demolish nothing, always add". While reflecting on my fascination with the area's self-built auto-repair workshops, "Demolish nothing, always add" should have been preceded by "Do not displace, welcome in". This marginal landscape of auto-parts, disaggregated and reassembled as precarious workshops and remodelled vehicles, was the result of situated work practices – lives that have since been displaced as part of contested urban renewal.

Cannon's reinterpretation of "Two Hundred Fifty Things an Architect Should Know" as a collective landscape endeavour brings a new dimension to this visionary work. From Kate Orff's contribution of "Bitches Get Stuff Done" to Aniket Bhagwat's "Understand the Soul of Derek Jarman", this book is both pragmatic advice and poetic demand. Although unable to include any of the landscape architects whom Michael listed in his "Two Hundred Fifty Things…" – "154. Capability Brown, André Le Nôtre, Frederick Law Olmsted, Musō Soseki, Ji Cheng and Roberto Burle Marx" – this is an extraordinary collection of lists that also includes delightful tensions and contradictions. In "Two Hundred Fifty Things a Landscape Architect Should Know" Cannon demonstrates his mastery in bringing landscape voices together, creating a true landscape list of lists.

Preface

B. Cannon Ivers

This book was spawned by loss and tragedy, but it is my hope that it will bring inspiration and optimism. When Michael Sorkin – the inimitable urbanist, theorist and architecture critic – died of COVID-19 on 26 March 2020, a groundswell of memories and commiserations filled social-media feeds, websites and design journals. It was also the first moment that the pandemic impacted someone whose work I followed and admired, a personality that I assumed floated above such eventualities as a global pandemic. Caught up in the collective reflection on Michael's work, I found myself reading his "Two Hundred Fifty Things an Architect Should Know", allowing each word to land with more profundity knowing that Sorkin was gone.

Motivated by this varied and far-reaching collection of thoughts, I immediately felt compelled to formulate a similar list – albeit through a diverse cohort of voices operating in the landscape architecture discipline. I envisioned an equally inspiring thread of observations, ideas, propositions and declarations expressed from the perspective of 50 landscape architects. The process of identifying, researching and assembling the contributors has been a once-in-a-lifetime experience. It has been an honour to work with each and every contributor, and to meet the personalities behind the widely recognised and celebrated work.

I first met Michael Sorkin when I was a student at Colorado State University. After witnessing his command of the English language and the range of his vocabulary, I recall commenting to my professor how astonished

I was by the number of words that I did not know from Sorkin's lecture. In a sagacious and professorial tone, my teacher, Merlyn Paulson, replied, "Remember, he learned each word one at a time." This has always stuck with me as a reminder that to really know a subject takes time and dedication. I hope the statements in this book reinforce this lesson. Each entry from the 50 contributors will have been learned and applied incrementally, in a particular context and over time – in some instances decades, or even an entire career. As observed by Anita Berrizbeitia, "Landscapes embody at once culture and nature, art and science, the collective and the personal, the natural and artificial, static and dynamic."[1] The medium is complex; the techniques and approaches are varied. It is my hope that this rare assemblage of inspired voices, operating in a myriad of contexts, will communicate the complexity, depth and interconnected qualities of the collective landscape project.

I am grateful to all of the contributors for the time and care they have committed to crafting their entries. I would like to thank the Birkhäuser team of Henriette Mueller-Stahl and Heike Strempel, to copy editor Ian McDonald and to graphic designer Lisa Petersen. A special thanks to Ed Wall for the generous foreword and the reflections on his personal and professional encounters with Michael Sorkin. Finally, to Jasper and Deelia, thank you for your ideas, you are wise beyond your years.

1   Czerniak, Julia (2001). *CASE: Downsview Park Toronto*. Cambridge, MA: Harvard University Graduate School of Design; Munich: Prestel p. 117.

The Complementarity of the Built and the Grown

We must understand that the built environment and the grown environment are complementary. Each has its own genesis, philosophy and aesthetic. Each adheres to its own laws, paradigms and orders. The built environment is the paradigm of structure, of rational order, of stable form; the grown environment is the paradigm of system, of the order of nature, of ever-changing matter. The built and the grown environments are complementary in that they are at once both interdependent and incomparable. Architecture that only consists of the built environment is ever only half-architecture; the same is true for the grown environment. One must never subjugate the other. Only when both are seen as equally important and equally necessary can we ever hope to achieve full and complete architecture.

1

Stig L. Andersson (SLA)
→ Copenhagen, Denmark

3

This villa by architect Arne Jacobsen radiates everything the built environment is based on: constructed order, hierarchy, repetition, stability. In the outdoor space, designed by the gardener and landscape architect G.N. Brandt, wild, complex, ever-changing life emerges. Here the built and the grown environment exist as each other's equal, forming a Whole Architecture. The collaboration made Jacobsen reflect that if he could choose a profession again he would opt to be a gardener. I exhibited this image from Brandt's archive in the Danish Pavilion at the 2014 Venice Architecture Biennale.

The New Nature is New

Many believe that nature-based design is about "reintro-ducing", "rewilding" or "reinstating" some kind of perceived "original nature" "back" into our cities. This is wrong. The New Nature that we are designing in our cities is not a copy of old romanticised images or idealised perceptions of nature past; the New Nature is truly new. We call this New Nature *City Nature*. It is man-made nature to correct man-made errors. It is a New Nature designed equally on the basis of deep *biological, anthropological, sociological* and *ecological* knowledge – and on a strong *artistic* know-ledge, experience and approach. It is a New Nature opti-mised to solve today's hardest urban challenges while creating genuine quality of life for humans. It is a New Nature that is not too concerned with how it *looks* – but rather how it *feels* and how it *functions*.

(2) Stig L. Andersson (SLA)
→ Copenhagen, Denmark

This artwork is in Copenhagen's Østerbro neighbourhood – a typical residential area, where everything that sprouts and grows is kept down, pruned, stemmed and maintained so as not to change or express living nature. Everything is controlled, following established norms and rules. We transformed the dominant infrastructure (roads, roundabouts, parking) into City Nature – a work of art with both economical and aesthetic utility value. Without reducing parking spaces, and optimised to handle the severest of cloudbursts and climate events, the neighbourhood is now enriched with the grown environment – with New Nature.

The Aesthetic Sense of Nature

Working with nature-based designs in our cities has a lot of advantages: the New Nature can strengthen biodiversity for plants and animals; its ecosystem services can handle a vast amount of our (self-inflicted) urban challenges like flooding, air pollution and microclimate challenges; and it can reduce stress, lifestyle diseases and mental and physical illness. These are all important; however, the *most* important aspect of working with nature in our cities is to bring the Aesthetic Sense of Nature to humans. The Aesthetic Sense of Nature is what all nature designs, and all nature designers, must aim for. It is the one thing *only* nature can bring. It is the realisation of all that is beautiful, strange, intimate, aesthetic, fascinating and frightening in nature. And it is the full sensory, physical, philosophical and aesthetic experience of nature – which, again, makes up our common human *ethical* foundation, and is thus one of the most fundamental and necessary experiences we as human beings can have.

(3) Stig L. Andersson (SLA)
→ Copenhagen, Denmark

During the years in which I lived in Japan, I became particularly aware of the value of Nordic Mannerism. I was intrigued by the manner in which the 19th-century Norwegian artist Peder Balke could feel the sublime in nature and make it comprehensible. He painted what he felt, not what he saw. He conceived the Aesthetic Sense of Nature in an aesthetic language, understood by emotions. He showed a path to the recognition of being a part of nature.

Humans *are* Nature

For centuries philosophers and scientists have discussed this most pressing of questions: are humans part of nature – or are we above or beside (or indeed beneath) it? One of the most important things a landscape architect must know is that humans are not only *part* of nature – we *are* nature. This insight is at once the simplest and also the most startling and disturbing insight that Modernity can imagine. If humans are nature, that means we must completely reconfigure the way we think about our presence in the world. Gone are the days when humans could subjugate nature in our attempts to reshape the world in our own image. Instead we must realise that we are here on this planet on equal terms with trees, plants, animals, jellyfish and mountains – an ethical knowledge that we must treat everything on Earth (the whole system of which we are part) in a decent way. We must take this knowledge seriously and make landscapes, cities and societies such as we have never seen before.

4 Stig L. Andersson (SLA)
→ Copenhagen, Denmark

When I first saw how the sculptor Gian Lorenzo Bernini's silky, soft, white and cold marble began to grow and transform into a barked and grouted olive tree with rough leaves (in order for his Daphne to avoid abuse at the hands of Apollo), I became aware that we are nature. I was in Rome in the early 1970s, and saw *Apollo and Daphne* in Villa Borghese. We humans are life, plants, stones and will – in constant transformation, metamorphosis and mutation.

Work Genuinely Interdisciplinarily

We must understand that creating something *truly* new is an interdisciplinary practice. Interdisciplinarity arises when many different professions are working together and equally on a common issue. Working in an interdisciplinary way is fundamental if we are to come up with new solutions and methods for our shared conditions. Working monodisciplinarily creates something we already know; working interdisciplinarily creates something we do not know yet. Therefore, the most important thing a landscape architect must realise is that we cannot do everything alone: we must engage with scientists, biologists, anthropologists, sociologists, humanists, ecologists, artists, literary scholars, philosophers – all different professions – in an equal and juxtaposed collaboration. The time for egos solving problems is gone – now is the time for truly collaborative work. Only together are we one.

(5) Stig L. Andersson (SLA)
→ Copenhagen, Denmark

As a student at Denmark's Technical University I learned how the physicist Niels Bohr developed his theories. He gathered people from different disciplines with a shared commitment to finding new ways to describe the world. This 1929 photograph shows Bohr, Wolfgang Pauli, Lothar Wolfgang Nordheim, Erwin Fues and Léon Rosenfeld. Outside the frame are Werner Heisenberg and Hendrik Kramers. During workshops Heisenberg blew a toy trumpet to give popular ideas a fanfare; Pauli, a cannon to shoot down unpopular ideas; and Kramers had a little drummer boy to provide applause.

The Capacity of Kigelia Africana to Sequester Carbon

Our future on Earth will be defined by two competing needs – the first, to accommodate a growing population; the second, to do so while inflicting little or no damage on our environments, ecologies or atmosphere. Without deep, landscape-led interdisciplinarity, we won't be able to keep up with the harm inflicted by our current typical building practices. How, then, should a landscape architect approach a site in the age of the Anthropocene – be it rural or urban, from 10 square metres to 100,000 hectares in size? The steps are simple: 1) conserve functioning ecologies; 2) restore ecological services; 3) proliferate biodiversity; and 4) sequester carbon. There can be no climate-positive architecture without complementary regenerative landscapes. And in five years' time, we must all be aware of both the carbon cost of every material we use, from concrete paving to anodised aluminium, and the carbon offset provided by everything we preserve or plant, from *Kigelia africana* to *Schizachyrium*.

6

Sierra Bainbridge (MASS)
→ Boston, MA, USA

Each *Kigelia africana* tree can sequester around 35,000 kilograms of carbon over its lifetime. Carbon-sequestration calculations are still developing, and even with tools like the Climate Positive Design Pathfinder so much of how we practise as landscape-systems designers cannot yet be accurately accounted for – such as soil and agricultural sequestration practices, or how they vary by continent. Through our work in Rwanda, we have started creating peer-reviewed calculations, which show that through inter-disciplinary collaboration we have designed possibly the world's first carbon-positive campus – on which we have preserved the *Kigelia africana* specimens.

How to See through Drawing

Our landscape is the most honest, earnest and unrelenting "keeper" of our shared histories. Recorded in decades and millennia, its embedded stories often remain hidden until we become able to decipher them. As landscape architects, we must learn material language and interpretative tools, helping to uncover the sometimes revelatory and sometimes terrible secrets that the landscape holds. We can see the hands that shaped it and the bodies held within it. A monocultural swathe, a tangle of pioneer weeds – if we look, we can see the story of decades and centuries of disturbances, transmigrations, transplantings and interminglings. Drawing from observation is the first lesson: Sit and draw what you see. If we can just begin to observe our landscape, it will reveal undeniable truths: first, we see the natural processes at work; then, we notice the species that are changing or marking change – we see actions and events, perpetrated both by nature and humanity. The land bears record of our deeds and misdeeds. To draw is to see. To draw is to record. Then, we can hold ourselves accountable.

(7) Sierra Bainbridge (MASS)
→ Boston, MA, USA

The pine plantations of the American South reveal a long-term shift from the region's labour-intensive cotton crop to a comparatively low-labour alternative. This process began after the abolition of slavery and intensified when, for many, continuing to farm in the South during the Jim Crow era became untenable. The pine tracts you pass through when driving west from Georgia to east Texas bear witness to the loss of forced and coerced labour.

About Jainism

Jainism is a centuries-old Indian religion teaching a path to spiritual purity and enlightenment through disciplined nonviolence. One of its key principles – *ahimsa* – means, in the original Sanskrit, "non-injury" to all living creatures.

COVID-19 has revealed the opposite: a cycle of injury that begets more injury. No fewer than 75% of new or emerging infectious diseases in people come from animals. This rate of zoonotic transmission is accelerating due to increasing human population and pressures on the environment, including extractive agricultural practices, rapid urbanisation and unprecedented human migration – all exacerbated by a rapidly changing climate. What if we designed as if we were Jains? We would do so in a way that values all forms of life and replenishes our ecological system. Designing for One Health – which acknowledges that human, animal and ecological health are inextricably linked – provides just such a framework for decision-making that accounts for carbon positivity, social equity and planetary health.

(8) Sierra Bainbridge (MASS)
→ Boston, MA, USA

The Rwanda Institute for Conservation Agriculture (RICA) was purpose-built to demonstrate the unique One Health pedagogy pioneered by the faculty. In the design of its landscape, buildings and infrastructure, we thought holistically about the materials we sourced; where and how and by whom they were extracted, harvested and made. Each of these moments become legible expressions of the principles of One Health, equity and stewardship.

The Fourteen Senses

Marginalised, "subaltern" or oppressed communities all emanate from the non-reflexive lens, which prioritises the world views of the mainstream, the coloniser, the oppressor. These embedded predilections create spaces that, at best, do not welcome or make comfortable a diversity of users and, at worst, systematically destroy the structures and networks that historically provided for the non-majority's needs. What happens when we push against that world view? When we centre instead the deaf, the indigenous, the immigrant, the blind and the Black experience? We learn how people of wide-ranging abilities and backgrounds feel, smell, touch, remember and navigate the landscape, and we can create a responsive, intentional design that, in serving their needs first, enriches all our experiences.

In so doing, we may gain the opportunity to investigate, reveal and coax out what can be called a "sixth sense," known by some as the magical sense. Temporal, phenomenological, seasonal and sensory aspects of perception lend themselves to creating experiences that can be transformative, invigorating and life affirming. Whether we are acculturated to having five, six or fourteen of them—as landscape architects, we must learn to design for all our senses.

(9) Sierra Bainbridge (MASS)
→ Boston, MA, USA

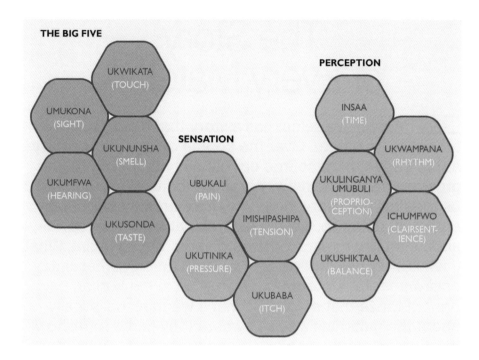

THE BIG FIVE

UKWIKATA
(TOUCH)

UMUKONA
(SIGHT)

UKUNUNSHA
(SMELL)

UKUMFWA
(HEARING)

UKUSONDA
(TASTE)

SENSATION

UBUKALI
(PAIN)

IMISHIPASHIPA
(TENSION)

UKUTINIKA
(PRESSURE)

UKUBABA
(ITCH)

PERCEPTION

INSAA
(TIME)

UKWAMPANA
(RHYTHM)

UKULINGANYA
UMUBULI
(PROPRIO-
CEPTION)

ICHUMFWO
(CLAIRSENT-
IENCE)

UKUSHIKTALA
(BALANCE)

Our senses are essential to our social and cultural understanding. Many cultures channel the world through the five senses, yet the ability to perceive our surroundings through our eyes, ears, nose, skin and mouth can be expanded. In Zambian traditional practice, there are fourteen senses, providing a deep and layered engagement with the natural world that incorporates dynamic forces and internal perceptions. Sensory experience is how knowledge is understood, remembered and transferred. This diagram reflects the indigenous knowledge as shared by Samba Yonga and Mulenga Kapwepwe, co-founders of the Women's History Museum in Zambia.

The Story of Every Material

Every material we select has a story that binds us to each other and to nature. Over the course of the 20th century, as we began to outsource our capacity to make and to grow, we traded the networks of production that had bound us together for ever-longer and more anonymous supply chains. In doing so, we ceased to be able to track our accountability to each other and to our environment. What if with every design decision, we ask not only what is the environmental footprint but also what is the human hand-print of those that made it? What if we think holistically about the materials we use – where they come from; how they are extracted, harvested and propagated; who manufactures, transports, assembles or grows them? While not every material can be local, many can. When we choose a local material, we have the potential to create ownership, familiarity, relationships and livelihoods. We also increase our ability to more easily observe, track, minimise or offset the damage to our communities and environment inflicted by typical material procurement.

(10)   Sierra Bainbridge (MASS)
→ Boston, MA, USA

Clockwise from top right:
1) Jean Baptiste has worked on five projects with MASS, propagating, planting and tending healing landscapes.
2) Anne Marie was trained in volcanic masonry. She is now working on her fifth project with MASS with the all-women masonry crew she founded.
3) At RICA we propagated and planted over 150,000 woodland savannah plants from species collected on site, demonstrating the crucial link between biodiverse ecologies and thriving agriculture.
4) Working with biologists from The Dian Fossey Gorilla Fund, we collected and propagated over 200,000 Afromontane species for educational, research and reforestation sitework.

The Price of Blooming the Desert

Our landscape designs are dependent on water resources and affect the water cycle. Thus, we need to be aware, and critical, of how waterscapes reflect political processes and ideologies. Massive hydraulic projects across the world that were built with the intention of "blooming the desert" were, and to a large extent still are, mainly the creation of nation states, and reflect their objectives.

The Jordan River flows from the Hula Valley to the Sea of Galilee, and from there to the Dead Sea. Its basin is split by the political borders of Lebanon, Syria, Israel, Jordan and the Palestinian National Authority. Israel controls the amount of water flowing into the Jordan River via a dam at the southern tip of the Sea of Galilee, the state's largest source of water. This made the Israeli national project of irrigating arid areas possible. It also dried up water resources shared by neighbouring countries and led to disastrous environmental outcomes.

11

Yael Bar-Maor
→ Tel Aviv, Israel

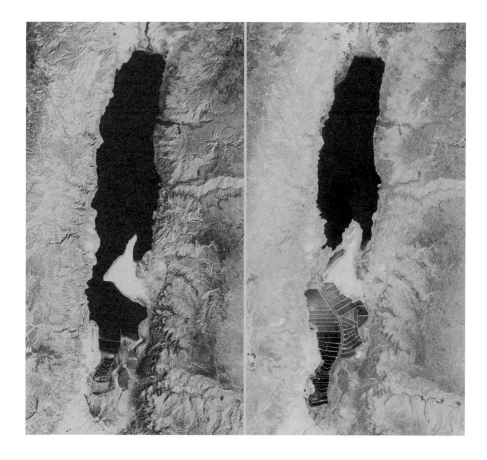

The Dead Sea transformation, 1972/2019
The Dead Sea is dying. It is constantly shrinking. Water levels are falling at a rate of over one metre per year, and its surface area has dropped from around 1,000 to 600 square kilometres in the past 70 years. A critical analysis of the Jordan River Basin waterscape prompts us to reject the way the concept of the human domination of nature is still being practised as part of efforts by nation states to gain power and control over natural resources, and to question the ethos of "blooming the desert".

The Course of a Raindrop

Waterscapes are landscapes viewed through the lens of their water resources, taken as a defining element of both ecosystems and human life.[1]

Reading and writing the terrain are among the most important skills of landscape architects. The best way to obtain these skills is by looking at landscapes through the lens of their water flow. By imagining the course of a raindrop on the ground, we can understand the forms and features of the topography of a site and envisage its potential transformation through our design.

The Arava Valley, north of Aqaba and Eilat, is a unique and fragile desert. Rainfall events in this area, however rare, can cause flash floods that have significant landscape-forming effects. Very few species of tree grow in these extreme conditions. Those that do include acacias, the valley's keystone species, which can, however, survive only where water flows through in episodic floods. Any human intervention in the topography shifts the surface water, and may change the trajectory and the effects of the floods. Working in this hyper-arid landscape reminds us of how sensitive we must be to the course of a single raindrop.

(12) Yael Bar-Maor
→ Tel Aviv, Israel

The Hanging Trees near Eilat, Israel, 2015
An abandoned quarry near Eilat is known for its "Hanging Trees": these native acacias are designated a protected species. During the quarry's working life, they were left untouched as the surrounding soil was excavated, leaving them stranded far above the flooding areas – a death sentence to most of them. When we were commissioned to plan the rehabilitation of the area, we decided to keep the dead trees in place as "anchors" helping us to understand the area's former topography, and as reminders of the responsibility that we owe to waterscapes.

1   Molle, François, Foran, Tira and Floch, Philippe (2009). "Introduction: Changing waterscapes in the Mekong region – Historical background and context", in François Molle, Tira Foran and Mira Käkönen (eds.). *Contested waterscapes in the Mekong region: Hydropower, livelihoods and governance.* London: Earthscan, p. 2.

The Kibbutz (as a Utopian Model)

Imagine a society of absolute sharing, where private property does not exist: a society that provides for all the material and social needs of its members. Every child growing up there gets an equal education, beginning at birth. Since everything is shared, there is no need for fences or divisions. The family-based household is irrelevant, for there is no private property to be handed down within the family and domestic functions are shared by the community.

What would the habitat of this society look like? What role could landscape play in such a place? The planners of the kibbutz tried to answer these questions, by giving form to this utopia. The first kibbutzim (plural form of kibbutz) were built a century ago in Palestine/Israel as collective settlements based on full partnership in all aspects of life. Over the years they developed a unique spatial typology that reflected the idea of total collectiveness, and set the stage for the everyday practices of communal life in which landscape played a leading role.

13

Yael Bar-Maor
→ Tel Aviv, Israel

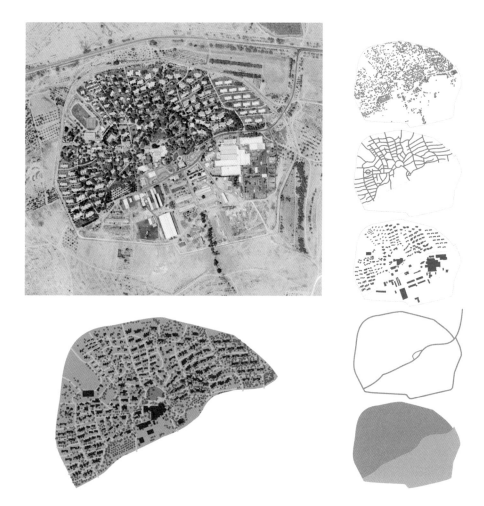

Spatial analysis of Kibbutz Hatzerim, Israel,
one of the few kibbutzim that still preserve a
cooperative system
The kibbutz as a whole was considered the home of
all its members. There were no private houses but
functional buildings, connected by footpaths and open
spaces, served as "rooms" across a continuous garden-
scape. Everyday practices – eating, playing, sometimes
even bathing – took place in communal spaces. The
utopian totality of togetherness became a dystopian
experience for some. Privatisation processes, starting
in the 1980s, gradually eliminated the various aspects
of communal life. Nevertheless, the kibbutz in its original form provides a fascinating case study in connections between spatial and social arrangements.

Planting is Political

Nik Heynen, Maria Kaika and Erik Swyngedouw's "'Manifesto' for Urban Political Ecology" states that "[t]he type and character of physical and environmental change, and the resulting environmental conditions, are not independent from specific historical, cultural, political or economic conditions and the institutions that accompany them".[1]

Sure enough, the Israeli-Palestinian conflict has a botanical aspect. Actions such as planting, uprooting, preferring one species over the other and even nature-protection laws reflect the conflict and impact on it. Perhaps the most notable of these actions is the massive foresting of lands nationalised by the state of Israel in the 1950s, previously belonging to Palestinians who fled or were forced out of their villages during the 1948 war. This transformed large parts of the country into coniferous forests, comprising mainly pines. The main objectives of this foresting action were political-tactical (obtaining control over the land) and economic (forestry as a workfare programme for incoming Jewish immigrants). At the same time it was an act of erasing the previous landscape, with all its cultural meaning, and introducing a new monoculture landscape that was meant to represent the "melting pot" of the newly founded state.

(14) Yael Bar-Maor
→ Tel Aviv, Israel

Monoculture pine forest vs. diverse vegetation
of local species proposed for a public grove,
the Galilee region, Israel
The act of planting and the choice of trees we plant
have cultural and political meaning, as well as environmental impact. Working on cross-cultural and cross-
sector cooperation projects also generates diversity in
planting choice. Being involved in projects in Galilee,
an area of mixed Arab and Jewish population, I am re-
introducing native species or those typical of the traditional cultivated areas that are now less common ow-
ing to top-down forestry and urbanisation. I see this as
increasing biodiversity and at the same time reflecting
the cultural diversity of the area.

1   Heynen, Nik; Kaika, Maria and Swyngedouw,
Erik (2006). "Urban political ecology: Politicizing the
production of urban natures", In the The Nature of
Cities; Urban Political Ecology and the Politics of Urban
Metabolism. Abingdon, UK: Routledge, p. 12.

What is Absent from the Map

Maps don't merely inform; they propose. They don't offer a neutral representation of reality; they construct reality in a particular way.[1]

It is extremely important to be aware of the subjective nature of mapping. Official maps often exclude data that do not correspond to the hegemonic policy. Such is the case of the Bedouin village Bir Hadaj in the Negev Desert. A few years ago, we received a commission from a governmental fund to design the rehabilitation of an abandoned quarry in "an open area" outside the village boundaries. But a visit to the site before starting the design process made it clear that we would be working at the heart of the village. The state recognises only around a third of the actual inhabited area, and most of it is absent from the statutory maps. We decided to put aside the official data and base our design on aerial photos, field trips and local knowledge obtained from the residents.

15

Yael Bar-Maor
→ Tel Aviv, Israel

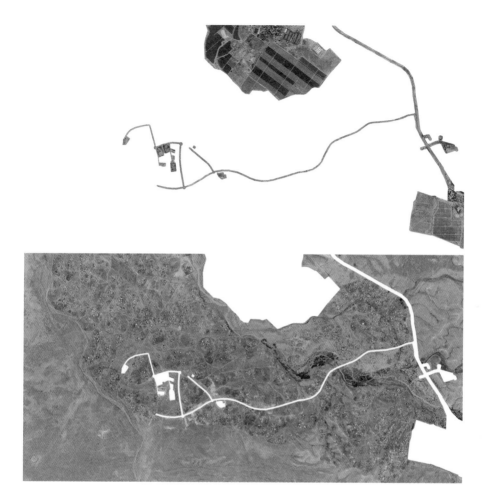

Formal vs. informal building and development,
Bir Hadaj and Revivim, the Negev region, Israel
Bīr Hadaj's residents were relocated by Israel's military
authorities in the 1950s. In the 1990s, after a hazard-
ous-waste disposal facility was developed near the
area to which they were transferred, they returned to
the vicinity of their historical home. The Israeli Government recognised the village, but only on a third of its
area. Maps construct reality. Being absent from them
means being denied basic rights. Citizens of the
Bedouin "diaspora" and non-governmental organisations working with them are using counter-mapping to
shed light on what has been left off the official maps.

1   Paez, Roger (2019). *Operative Mapping;
Maps as Design Tools*. Barcelona: Elisava, p. 9.

Be in the Landscape

Visit landscapes and experience them, and actively critique the way you interpret that experience. Visit natural, modified and human-designed places. Go back to your old projects and learn from their ageing. If you are travelling, research ahead and make an itinerary and be open to all the places not on that itinerary. Don't believe published images. The hero-shot can be a profound evil. Projects have context, need to be seen in sun and rain and crowds and at night and when you're lonely or feeling like a hard-arsed eco-warrior. Capture your experiences. The first moment. Shifting impressions over time. Detail. The broader surrounds. Then be disciplined and file those photos or notes or drawings or sound recordings with the right names or tags. This is a practice that will give and give for your whole career.

16

Kirsten Bauer (ASPECT Studios)
→ Victoria, Australia

National Emergency Services Memorial,
Canberra, Australia, 2004
The on-site design of the National Emergency Services
Memorial, using a simple 1:1 string model, developed
the memorial's play of horizon line, topography, scale

and approach. This was an early success at ASPECT
Studios, and each time I revisit and photograph this
project my attention is drawn to different things: the
mountains, the shadows, the trees and its ageing as it
settles into its landscape. Designers: ASPECT Studios

Everything is Design

Sure, design can be the grand gesture. But don't let anyone tell you documenting a project is not design. It all is. Design is how you craft every moment of every project. A path is not a path – it's a material, a journey, a pattern, a tension created with purpose and referencing a rich typology. "See a world in a grain of sand", as Blake said.[1] Bring everything you can to whatever is before you and imagine yourself in everything you design. Extend that to see through others' eyes. And extend that to see beyond simply the human: as Claude Lévi-Strauss famously said, animals are "good to think [with]".[2] Design is an attitude as well as a craft.

(17)   Kirsten Bauer (ASPECT Studios)
→ Victoria, Australia

Caulfield to Dandenong railway project and
Djerring Trail, Melbourne, Australia, 2019
A shared pathway orchestrates the complex chain of
civic, play, rest, fitness and gathering spaces along the
17 kilometres of linear parkland created as part of the
Caulfield to Dandenong railway project. The narrow corridor, just 20–40 metres wide, created by the elevation
of the rail line, now unites communities, strengthens local identity, drives urban regeneration, promotes non-
car travel and provides essential urban habitat and
connection to nature. Designers: ASPECT Studios and
Cox Architecture

1   Blake, William (1950). "Auguries of innocence",
in Auden, W. H., and Norman H. Pearson (eds.). *Poets of
the English language*, vol. 4. New York: Viking.

2   Lévi-Strauss, Claude (1963). *Totemism*.
Boston: Beacon Press, p. 89.

Earth, Water, Plants and Time

These are fundamental to landscape. Designers often move too quickly to walls, seats, paving – and miss the power these fundamentals possess. Earth literally grounds us, and means landform, sculpting and texture. Soils are living materials and can make or break a project. Few landscape architects know soils well. Water means life, a most profound material to work with. Water play, microclimate, as "white noise" softening a busy road, essential resource, flood management, reflection: it has a thousand aspects. Plants are immensely important. What a single tree can do in terms of ecosystem services is incredible. Plants are aesthetically subtle, culturally profound, ecologically essential and do much to create human health and wellbeing. Our projects are never finished; they exist in time. As they mature others guide them towards a future we have designed. You can easily spend a lifetime learning to use these fundamentals well.

18   Kirsten Bauer (ASPECT Studios)
      → Victoria, Australia

Victorian Desalination Plant Reserve,
Wonthaggi, VIC, Australia, 2012
The design of the Victorian Desalination Plant Reserve
was driven by the need to minimise the visual bulk of
the water factory and to accommodate millions of cubic
metres of spoil. ASPECT's topographic response used
grades of spoil to construct an artificial dunal system
and a vast green roof – both of which provided the basis
for the transformation of depauperate farmland into a
rich, self-sustaining mosaic of vegetation and wetlands
based on the site's original coastal ecosystems. Designers: ASPECT Studios, Practical Ecology, ARM Architecture and peckvonhartel

Representation Matters

How you choose to draw or represent a site will influence how you design the site and how you think about your design, so choose wisely. We use representation to think through design, to explore, to communicate not just with others but to ourselves. If you think through plan, you may lose spatiality. If you think through 3D form, you may lose a cultural narrative. Diagrams may abstract ideas that are better given form through planting. Drone-style animation fly-throughs may impress a client but communicate little of the on-ground experience. Each mode of representation brings its own limits and biases. Know these. Don't get sucked in by your own artifice. Don't confuse the images you use to sell a project with the images you use to create a project. The gap between them can swallow you alive.

19   Kirsten Bauer (ASPECT Studios)
→ Victoria, Australia

Bunurong Memorial Park, Bangholme,
VIC, Australia, 2016
While the aspiration for Bunurong Memorial Park was
to create a contemporary cemetery, its design was
much influenced by the mapping of burial-plot price
as a function of its view to water. The relationship
between topography and value meant mounding became crucial. To represent the cemetery as a place
for the living, ASPECT placed a playground at the
cemetery's entrance. Further detailed design required
understanding the physical dimensions of cemetery
"product", such as the containers used for cremains.
Designers: ASPECT Studios and BVN Architecture

Landscape Architecture is a Political and Cultural Act

Landscape is a cultural construct. What we do and how we do it constitutes a political act that will affect people and this planet. The consequences of our actions are sometimes subtle, sometimes blunt – but always pervasive. We are not passive. We are agents of change. Landscape architecture is enacted in the public domain, and we have a moral responsibility not just to our clients but to the environment and the community. Our job is often to make a bad project better – for example, a development replacing a well-treed neighbourhood or greening a freeway. Often we must educate and guide our clients, find the local government policies that back our arguments, offer a change in perspective. Often we have to cajole our clients into becoming better human beings, sometimes we subtly subvert them, occasionally we even have to fight them. Always remember, the return brief is mightier than the sword.

20 Kirsten Bauer (ASPECT Studios)
→ Victoria, Australia

Yagan Square, Perth, Australia, 2018
Yagan Square rethinks the city's heart. The design process committed to collaboration with Traditional Owners to allow many stories of place to emerge, both indigenous and post-colonial; to celebrate supressed histories of the city, its people and landscape. In doing so, normative spatial models were discarded while the functional complexities of the brief were embraced by new forms that encourage reconciliation between Traditional Owners and colonialists following two centuries of oppression. Designers: Lyons Architecture in collaboration with ASPECT Studios and iredale pederson hook architects

Landscapes Obscure[1]

Context is a critical variable in landscape architecture, but it is often reduced to what is immediately visible. Landscape architects should look beyond what they see in order to unveil the forces that drive the evolution of a place, whether a garden or a territory, at multiple scales. These include known and forgotten environmental and social histories that explain the present, as well as intentionally erased histories of oppression and conflict; of extraction; and other forms of ecological exploitation, disinvestment and neglect.

The issue, however, is not only about exposing how landscape works as a repository of both human enlightenment and abuse but also about how to keep this consciousness in everyday practice. Landscape architects should know what their renderings hide, which narratives are left out of the pastoral depictions of their designs. To aspire to contribute towards a socially and environmentally just world entails designs, and their representations, that reveal what is hidden behind the view.

21

Anita Berrizbeitia
→ Cambridge, MA, USA

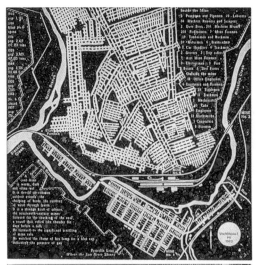

Vintondale Reclamation Park, Vintondale, PA, USA
Julie Bargmann and Stacy Levy, 1996
Above: Plan of the Vintondale, PA coal mine, showing a
fraction of the extensive network of tunnels north of
the town. The texts show the human dimension of
the mines: statistics of individuals in the workforce, a
poem that registers the life of the mine. Galvanised
metal case, glass plate, coal gathered at the site.
Below: Reclamation Site Plan, 1996. The series of tri-
angular pools comprises the passive treatment system
for the acid mine drainage. The system was carved out
of the abandoned coke works on the floodplain of the
Blacklick River.

1   Mitchell, Don (2008). "New Axioms for Reading
the Landscape: Paying Attention to Political Economy
and Social Justice", in James L. Wescoat Jr and
Douglas M. Johnston (eds.). *Political Economies of
Landscape Change, Places of Integrative Power*.
Dordrecht: Springer, p. 33.

The Universal in the Local

All landscapes operate at multiple scales. The sections of Alexander von Humboldt and Patrick Geddes are key examples of multiscalar thinking. Humboldt sought to explain how, even though the Earth's rocky crust had been formed by the same set of geological processes throughout, the life forms that covered that crust changed dramatically depending on local conditions. Embracing a planetary perspective, he developed sectional drawings that contained multiple layers of geographical information, integrating diverse systems of knowledge in one image.

In his *Valley Section* Patrick Geddes explains the relationship between universal principles and processes and local conditions. Utilising, like Humboldt, the idea of the transect, the section is a conceptual diagram that describes how natural resources support early forms of human settlement and the eventual formation of cities.

To address climate change, landscape architects will need to integrate systems of knowledge, and express the interrelatedness of things across scales of time, place, space, region and territory.

22   Anita Berrizbeitia
→ Cambridge, MA, USA

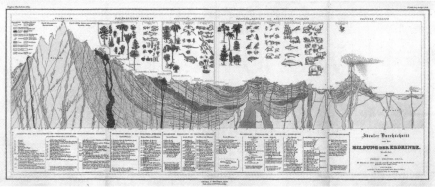

Above: Alexander von Humboldt (1769–1859), Diagram of a cross-section of the Earth's crust, 1841, in Berghaus, Heinrich (1852). *Physikalischer Atlas*. Gotha: J. Perthes. The cross section shows the underlying geology of the Earth's surface and how the composition of plant and animal species changes along the transect from ocean to mountain top.

Below: Sir Patrick Geddes (1854–1932), *Valley Section*, 1910. Geddes introduced the concept of the region as the basic analytical framework that explained the mutually dependent relationship between geographical areas – as a fount of resources – and the formation of cities.

Cities: Why, How and for Whom?

In one sense, all cities are the same: they are "socio-economic attractors"[1] that, much like organisms, require inputs (energy, water, food, materials, capital, labour etc.); produce outputs (commodities, waste, transportation, social relations etc.); need infrastructure to facilitate and manage both; and evolve through time. Yet no two cities are the same, and the differences are most clearly seen in their forms and in the relationship of those forms to the many functions they serve. Knowing the differences matters because it brings into sharp focus how and why form, spaces and materials shape the experience of a city and determine its ability to function sustainably and in an equitable way.

To understand how differences arise, it is necessary to know how cities were built and why, what the environmental and social histories behind them are, who they were designed for, who was left out, what motivated change, how they are funded, and the extent of networks that sustain them.

(23) Anita Berrizbeitia
→ Cambridge, MA, USA

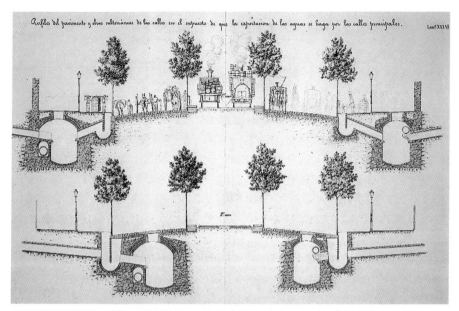

Fig. 29.

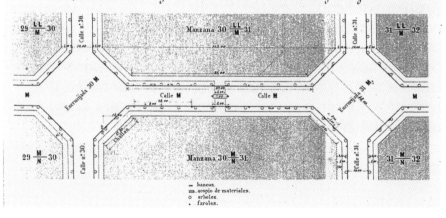

Ildefons Cerdà (1815–1876), details for the
expansion plan of Barcelona, Spain, 1859
Above: Cross-section of streets showing mobility, street
tree planting and underground drainage system.
Below: Detail plan of street intersections for the expansion plan of Barcelona. Principles that promoted the
need for sunlight, natural lighting and ventilation in
cities formed part of several criteria behind the form
of the plan.

1   West, Geoffrey and Bettencourt, Luis (2014).
"What is a City", The Atlantic, 3 September.
https://www.theatlantic.com/video/index/380650/
what-is-a-city (accessed 15.02.2021).

How to be a "Complete Designer"

I invoke here the entire legacy of Roberto Burle Marx rather than a specific work, lecture or his activities as a plant collector and propagator. Burle Marx was a polymath: his engagement with the visual and design arts ran as deep as that with horticulture and ecology, with grassroots advocacy and high-level politics. During the time and place in which he worked – Brazil in a period of accelerated economic growth and environmental degradation – separating out any of these many strands would have been inconceivable.

As landscape architects become more focused on "problem-solving", they risk losing their capacity to become "complete designers". Literacy, if not proficiency, in other cultural, visual or spatial practices is necessary in order to keep their work responsive – and relevant – to the world around them. Equally important is a knowledge of how policy intersects with design. Burle Marx knew and utilised the success and visibility of his work – aesthetically, socially, ecologically – in the political arena for the greater public and environmental good.

(24) Anita Berrizbeitia
→ Cambridge, MA, USA

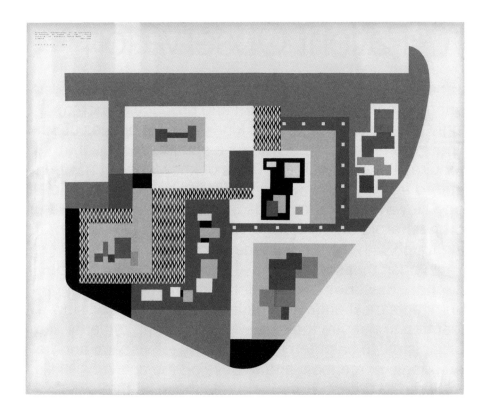

Roberto Burle Marx (1909–1994),
Detail No. 5 of plan for Quadricentennial Gardens,
Ibirapuera Park, São Paulo, Brazil, 1953
Burle Marx was formed in the tradition of Latin American Modernism that called for the integration of the arts, in which design was conceived as a synthetic whole – comprising, in equal parts, sculpture, painting and volumetric space. A versatile designer, he practised – in addition to landscape architecture – painting, print-making, jewellery making and fabric design. Between 1967 and 1974 he served in the government's Federal Council of Culture, advocating for the protection of the environment.[1]

1   Seavitt Nordenson, Catherine (2018). *Depositions. Roberto Burle Marx and Public Landscapes under Dictatorship.* Austin: University of Texas Press.

Patient Observation

Landscape is slow. Learning it is even slower. Yet the present moment forces us to learn and produce at increasingly greater speeds, with all kinds of technologies at our fingertips (literally) to do so. As a spatial practice that requires the input of many fields of knowledge, it has benefitted from the integration facilitated by digital technology. However, it places landscape architects in the role of orchestrators of knowledge, of generalists at risk of losing touch with the medium they work with.

I posit that some forms of knowledge in landscape cannot – must not – be accelerated, and that landscape architects must engage in patient observation and slow learning to deepen their knowledge of living systems and organisms, to heighten their capacity for visceral and emotional perception, and to develop the analytical skills required to detect orders and relationships that can potentially be translated into the design of exceptional experiences and places.

25

Anita Berrizbeitia
→ Cambridge, MA, USA

THIRTEEN WAYS OF LOOKING AT A BIRCH *(for Wallace Stevens)*

I *Taxonomically* II *Botanically* III *Geobotanically* IV *Morphologically* V *Spatially* VI *Atmospherically* VII *Acoustically* VIII *Biochemically* IX *Ec...ologically* X *Phenologically* XI *Ethnobotanically* XII *Economically* XIII *Horticulturally*

Mara K. Smaby,
"Thirteen Ways of Looking at a Birch", 2021
Above: Omar Hoftun, *Betula utilis subsp. albosinensis
seeds*, 2016.
Below: Giovanna Bernetti/EUFORGEN, Illustration of
Betula pendula seed, 2009.

Understand the Soul of Derek Jarman

He died in 1994.
Of his impending death he knew well.
Walking often on an inhospitable beach, made macabre by a
nuclear power station, he picked
driftwood and small plants gasping for breath.
At his cottage he arranged them and nurtured all that he saw.
The flowers peeped out ever so
tentatively, and showed themselves to the world. They survive.
He did this with passion till the end.
He knew he was dying, but did not falter. And in doing so he found life.
In a world that seems to hurtle towards an unwelcome environmental,
social and cultural outcome,
where an individual seems ineffectual – remember him.
Let us be ordained to tell the story of life and the wondrous ideas
of nature, irrespective of the
outcome.
Or if we will see the results of our efforts. He did not care.

26 Aniket Bhagwat
→ Ahmedabad, India

Conscious of one's mortality, one begins to tend to the neglected ones, the dying ones – the orphans – and give them a new life. In the harshness of the English coast, by the towering nuclear power station, he arranges flint and rocks, driftwood and found objects. A garden emerges in the desolate, barren landscape.

Life is Not Complete without Spending a Winter Day at Nishat Baugh

Envious, the emperor ordered they not survive,
A caring gardener defied
Turned the water on,
The gardens bloomed.
That is Kashmir.
Twelve terraces, each a celestial sign
One approaches from the lake,
Slowly the stately chinar trees rise and compress space
The plains fall behind, the valley constricts.
That is Kashmir.
And within the green walls of shadow and texture,
The terraces rise,
Each leaving a world behind,
Till at last, the mountains engulf.
That is Kashmir.
A land where, water desiccates land.
Sometimes still, and then it gurgles and splashes,
Held in narrow streams and at other times in large pools.
A moment, held between the mountains and water.
That is Kashmir.
Of still winters, without the showy babble,
Internalising the despair, and yet a stoic majestic calm,
Of grace, kindness humanity and forgiveness,
That denies a scarred soul.
That is Kashmir.

27 Aniket Bhagwat
→ Ahmedabad, India

Perched on the edge of the Dal Lake, and framing the magnificent Zabarwan Mountains, offering commanding views of the Pir Panjal mountain range, the gardens of Nishat Baugh resonate deeply with the valley of Kashmir. As the large chinar trees become manifestations of the mountains, as the water flows through, the gardens reflect the spirit of Kashmir.

Gardens are the Last Political Spaces on the Planet

The eyes don't leave us.
On the streets, in schools, colleges, malls, theatres and offices.
Even at times in homes.
We are always in places of many contestations;
having to negotiate our place in the world.
Some of us strive to express sexuality; others want equality in race;
yet others rue the world of economic disparity.
Some are just bullied because they don't fit;
others are oppressed, their rights
trampled.
Bosses, politicians, police, parents, spouses, children,
owners, landlords, warlords, overbearing
friends – the list is endless.
And then we enter a garden. The chains melt and recede. We can be.
We can be whoever we wish – a king, a joker, a bird, a cloud,
a spring, a flower, a raindrop, a
dreamer, a poet, a cookie;
the list is endless.
Gardens are oysters. They don't judge, and let specks become.

28
Aniket Bhagwat
→ Ahmedabad, India

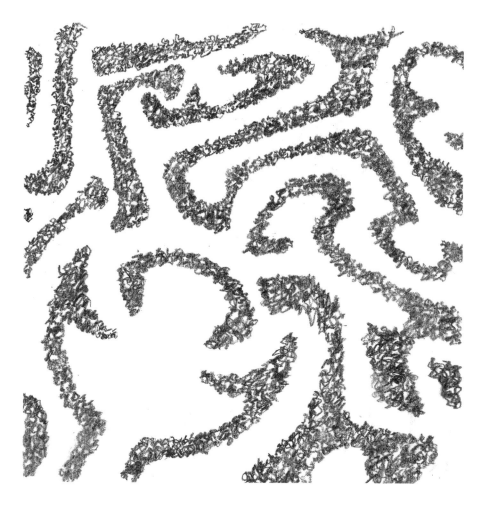

Amidst tall grass, amidst fragrant flowers, under the shade of the trees or over the soft rolling lawns, one finds oneself, relieved of expectations, relieved of judgement.

One is free. One is at peace. The garden is indeed the last political space on the planet.

The Schism between Landscape Gardeners and Landscape Architects is a Smokescreen

Like all mythical feuds the cause of this one is buried deep
in the hearts of men long gone.
Two tribes serve the same gods and yet dare not acknowledge the other.
One uses coded text and diagrams to determine the place of flowers;
the other stands amidst them,
and seats them in careful groups as one does with friends
at a dinner table.
One sits in darkened chambers, imagining the world of people,
and feverishly devises ways
of reconnecting them to many ideas of nature;
the other tramples in the open, observes with a
keen eye and brings that delight to man as simply as can.
One privately scorns all things small, the other revels in them
They both serve the same gods; Earth, Water, Air, All things living,
and their shrine is the
Garden.

29

Aniket Bhagwat
→ Ahmedabad, India

The catalogue of tools

Being a Divine Storyteller Who Speaks a Universal Language

Finally when it is all over, it's only the stories that remain.
We hear them when young. Morals are imbibed, lessons learned.
We gather them as we grow; tales of love, friendships, hardships
and how to counter them;
of greatness and of inspiration.
They accompany us as faithful companions;
silent till we wish them to speak.
Like warm clothes on a cold winter day, our lives are layered with them.
In a world numbed by the onslaught of mindless words and images,
honest powerful stories will
be remembered.
And if we want the world to heed us, we will have to learn to tell them.
Of cities and their memories, about the fragility and
delight of nature, of our culture and
of our place in the world and its meanings.
Every site a page, every project, many stories,
every element a chapter, a poem, or even a
soliloquy.

30

Aniket Bhagwat
→ Ahmedabad, India

The house sits on a large piece of farmland, with many orchards. Engaging with the mango trees, the chikoo trees, the rows of sandalwood and casuarina trees, the landscapes installed amidst the fields are sculptural, simple, yet dramatic – making cosmic connections between land and the celestial.

It's All about Great Bone Structure

No, we're not talking about Timothée Chalamet, Angelina Jolie or Catherine Deneuve. We're talking about cultural landscapes – both designed and vernacular – which have a purposeful shaping through planning, design, use and necessity. Understanding their inherent visual and spatial frameworks/constructs is essential when developing a site-sensitive and appropriate integration of form giving, place making and land shaping. A landscape's "bone structure" not only connects us with its past but also serves as the armature and inspiration when managing change with continuity.

31

Charles A. Birnbaum
→ Washington, DC, USA

The L'Enfant Plan (1791) and McMillan Plan (1902) establish the "bone structure" that informs planning and design decisions when managing change in Washington, DC's historic core.

There is no "A" in Olmsted, and He Didn't Live from 1822 to 1957

In fact, there were three. Frederick Law Olmsted Sr (1822–1903) defined and named the profession, and designed many of America's most beloved 19th-century parks and landscapes – including New York's Central Park, Brooklyn's Prospect Park and the US Capitol grounds. And then there was Frederick Law Olmsted Jr (1870–1957) and Senior's nephew (and then stepson) John Charles Olmsted (1852–1920). Their firm – Olmsted Brothers – designed park systems for several major cities – including Boston, Denver and Seattle. Beyond the Olmsted family, Warren Manning worked for Olmsted Sr; Dan Kiley worked for Manning; Gregg Bleam, who has just (as of 2020) contributed to the design for the Memorial to Enslaved Laborers at the University of Virginia, worked for Kiley. The story goes on. Why does this continuum of mentorship matter? It's important to know the mentors and muses that helped to shape these practitioners and others – because if we don't know where we've come from as a profession, how can we possibly know where we are going?

32

Charles A. Birnbaum
→ Washington, DC, USA

We all know that Frederick Law Olmsted Sr looked
tired, but he did not live from 1822 to 1957!

Landscape Architecture is More than "Parsley around the Roast"

The great Modernist landscape architect Thomas Church once quipped of the perceived relationship of landscape architecture to architecture that it's "parsley around the roast". Church's joke actually indicates an imbalance in perception based on a misunderstanding of the profession, which can have serious implications in the execution of projects. Landscape architects have a panoramic perspective, and they should have the opportunity to be involved early enough in a project in order to have maximum leverage in making and managing core planning and design decisions – yet they are often brought in late in the process. When should a landscape architect be engaged in a project? According to long-time landscape architect and professor William "Bill" Johnson, "early, early, early".

(33) Charles A. Birnbaum
→ Washington, DC, USA

The pioneering campus landscape design for the Weyerhaeuser International Headquarters by Sasaki, Walker and Associates, with Peter Walker as design lead, is more than mere decoration. The performative landscape architecture and Skidmore, Owings & Merrill's building architecture are seamlessly interwoven and symbiotic.

Making Public Landscapes Accessible to All is about More than just Issues of Expanding Edge, Porosity and Connectivity

Freedom of movement is an essential element and aspiration of our shared built environment, yet it is not a given and should not be taken for granted. Historically in the USA, segregation limited and prevented freedom of movement – on concerns ranging from passive and active recreation to the basic issue of where people were allowed to live and work. Even today, a person of colour can be attacked and killed simply for jogging in a residential neighbourhood. The concept of "race and space" and the very notion that freedom of movement was historically not available to all must be addressed in design, and not relegated to text and sign panels. Moreover, landscape architects have a key role to play in inviting, fostering and advancing creative ideas and welcoming site-specific solutions for all – and, in the process, making visible, and instilling value in, those sometimes forgotten stories and narratives.

(34) Charles A. Birnbaum
→ Washington, DC, USA

Although many US public parks were promoted as being open to all during the first half of the 20th century, they were rarely designed to the same standards for African Americans as they were for White people. At Chickasaw Park in Louisville, Kentucky the 1923 design by Olmsted Brothers afforded freedom of movement that was equally available to all.

You Cannot Design with Nature without Designing with Culture

Since the 1960s, landscape architects have been inculcated to recognise and give priority to natural and ecological systems as part of the design process. If we are to manage change in a landscape successfully, we must begin by recognising that our knowledge base for adequately assessing and quantifying the cultural value of landscape architecture is still developing. Questions about the cultural value of the designed urban landscape have moved from intellectual arguments in scholarly journals to debates in city councils, on editorial pages, in studios and classrooms, in the blogosphere, and elsewhere in the academic and public realm. We need to stand up, be advocates, and tell the stories we are crafting – in writing, verbally and using the full arsenal of artistic media that are available to us today (isn't that what Lawrence Halprin and Laurie Olin did so effectively to get their works built?). But more needs to be done; we need to be increasingly purposeful in advancing more holistic, systems-based approaches to problem solving and planning.

(35) Charles A. Birnbaum
→ Washington, DC, USA

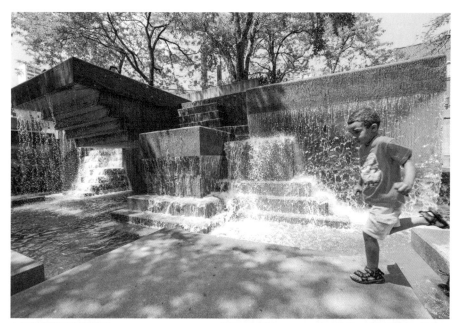

Landscape architecture has cultural value. The recent renewal of Peavey Plaza in Minneapolis, Minnesota (originally designed by M. Paul Friedberg in 1975 and rehabilitated by Coen+Partners in 2019) illustrates what successful change with continuity can look like. Top image 2008, bottom image 2021.

The Man-Made and the Natural are Often Pitted in Opposition[1]

As a landscape architect, a reasonable mediator between these two phenomena, your design should reconcile with a radical touch. To design is to draw out a plan that not only complies with the given ambitions but can also be resilient through time. The plan will most probably outlive its maker, and most designers are lucky to see their projects reach "puberty". Gardens and parks begin their lifespan at the moment of implementation, taking decades to grow to resemble the vision that nurtured them. The only constant for gardens, landscapes and the living entities that shape and inhabit them is change. Nature takes over, grows, seeds itself, multiplies; its roots invade new territories or it dies out and disappears. A radical, clear strategy will help solidify intent while allowing it to adjust fluidly to the effects of time. To protect the essence from being extinguished, work towards a design that can afford to surrender to spontaneity or reasonable adjustments by the owners.

36 Petra Blaisse (Inside Outside)
→ Amsterdam, The Netherlands

Competition design for the city of Antwerp, Belgium
© Inside Outside

1   See Treib, Marc (2005). *Settings and Stray Paths: Writings on Landscapes and Gardens.* New York: Routledge, p. 29.

A Landscape Does Not Belong to Itself

Landscape architecture is a service discipline, indebted to its future users: the client and the environment. It is shaped and defined by the context that breeds it. There is not a single element in the urban landscape that can exist on its own terms, and to attempt authorship over the landscape is to assume the role of a diplomat. Your vision will always have to develop wayfinding amidst a cloudy convolution of contradictory wishes, demands and regulations that will, at times, make the whole seem elusive. It will take patience and integrity to realise that these very interrelationships are as rhizomatic and entangled as the building blocks are with the landscape itself (and as root systems and fungi with one another). In landscape architecture, meaning is not inherent in singularity but fixed in the fluctuating relationship to external factors. It takes strategic talent, humour and a level of stubbornness to keep translating the complex pile of requested issues and impossibilities back into the basic and well-substantiated concept that you believe in with conviction.

(37) Petra Blaisse (Inside Outside)
→ Amsterdam, The Netherlands

Biblioteca degli Alberi in Milan, Italy
© Andrea Cherchii

We Like to Work upon and across the Threshold between Inside and Outside

Creating an exterior that is contoured by the intimacy of an interior is something of a traditional approach when it comes to creating gardens in a classical sense. There is something inherently hybrid about the interior world of an outside garden. But landscapes in an urban context do not necessarily have a close relationship to an interior, as they are impossible to isolate from the bigger picture. Nevertheless, as key players in urban developments, they need to pull together a city's architecture, intricate traffic and pedestrian networks, and underground infrastructure in an unconstrained manner. Thus, even large-scale urban landscapes can have an all-encompassing effect, tying the city together as one by having separate entities flow into each other or outward into the landscape outside the urban boundaries. The landscape is an active connector, and a welcome placeholder for developments to come.

Petra Blaisse (Inside Outside)
→ Amsterdam, The Netherlands

Seattle Central Library, Seattle, WA, USA
© Iwan Baan

Life as We Know it Begins and Ends in the Underground

It is home to the tiniest "springs and gears" of our natural world: the microscopic inhabitants of soil that impact on macroscopic ecologies. As movers and shakers of the natural world, landscape architects often seem reluctant to open up a blind eye towards the underworld, home to the age-old geological processes that are outside the purview of us mere mortals. But both its rapidly changing and geological natures form the foundation of our everyday life above ground. Abandon your creator complex and revel in all of the inner workings of a landscape that are already there, although initially invisible to the naked eye. Underground structures exacerbate the situation of the site in question: water levels can be pushed upwards, clog the natural flow and drainage, or limit air circulation. Collaborate with the slow and strategic processes of the mushroom; get to know the secret language between fungi and staggering root systems and the nesting, tunnel-digging animal life that opens up the base on which you work to necessary air and water retention …

(39) Petra Blaisse (Inside Outside)
→ Amsterdam, The Netherlands

Underground symbiosis
Your underground plot is essential in creating a new equilibrium between the built and the natural – between humans and nature. Pictured here is an underground symbiosis. The fungus ectomycorrhiza helps the roots of the pine to absorb nutrients. The fungi are microscopic – the width of this magnified image is, in reality, 3.5 millimetres. © Wim van Egmond

Maintenance is a Man-Made Landscape's Best Friend

But unfortunately, its importance is usually overlooked by clients, developers and architects. As landscape architects and designers, we need to trigger an attention to maintenance from the get-go. The future and quality of a place depends on it! Rather than short-term thinking in terms of new beginnings, a landscape requires long-term care. The level of ambition (not only in the sense of logistics and efficiency but also in understanding the value of life and beauty for wellbeing) and budget (in relation to its effect on surrounding property) go hand in hand. A landscape needs a professional gardener, whose mind understands and can keep up with the atmosphere of the changing seasons; who knows all about ground, root and plant life; and who takes pride in bringing a place to life and helping it thrive – while keeping an eye on its users.

40 Petra Blaisse (Inside Outside)
→ Amsterdam, The Netherlands

Landscape collage, conceptualisation
for the garden of the Stedelijk Museum in
Amsterdam, The Netherlands
© Petra Blaisse

Nothing is Flat

When I first met Kathryn and Neil,[1] Kathryn explained to me that the difference between landscape and architecture is that in the former discipline "nothing is flat". Having trained and practised as an architect I find the fact that nothing is flat or orthogonal in nature to be an obvious but profound thought. Our relationship with and perception of space changes as we move through a landscape. The body reads subtle changes in landform through movement. The eye looks for a horizon, the Earth, the sky. Topography defines place. Sectional drawings can be incredibly useful in exploring the spatial characteristics of a landscape. In today's digital world of 3D renders and virtual reality the section is often overlooked. The relationship between our eye height and the surrounding landscape can quickly be evaluated in a section. What is the sense of enclosure when standing? How does it change when sitting? How does space open up and reveal itself as one moves through it?

41 Mary Bowman (Gustafson Porter + Bowman)
→ London, United Kingdom

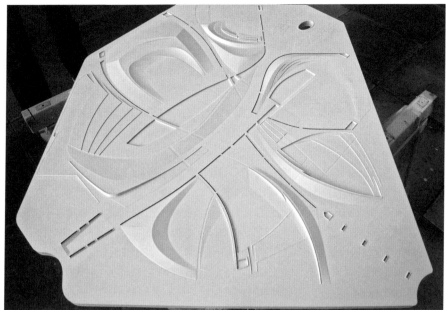

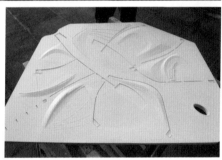

Parque Central, Valencia, Spain,
phase 1, 2011–ongoing
Our Central Park project in Valencia, Spain takes a relatively flat site, formerly occupied by railway lands, and
remodels its terrain to create a three-dimensional experience that references the hills, rivers, water channels and sea that surround the city. Through the creation of "bowls" or landforms – and the use of retaining
walls, steps and terraces – the Central Park transforms
an open, flat landscape into a series of distinct garden
spaces. Model by GP+B

1   Gustafson Porter + Bowman was established
in 1997 when landscape architect Kathryn Gustafson
opened a London office with architect Neil Porter.
Mary Bowman joined the practice in 2002.

Not All Ground is the Same

You need to understand your context and your site – there is a huge impact from both the unseen and the unforeseen (soil conditions, pollution, services, archaeology etc.). The secret is to integrate the landscape effortlessly and seamlessly with the urban fabric that surrounds the site. One should never discuss, change or design a landscape without visiting it first – climate, topography, flora and fauna, as well as human social interactions and cultural influences, create the dialogue that helps develop a relevant and meaningful response. Understand the relationship between human habitation and the natural world: how do we allow for cultural interaction while protecting the natural environment and allowing for biodiversity? Every site is unique. Cultural, historical and environmental conditions make each project special and are the starting point for your conceptual approach to design. Learn from your colleagues in other disciplines – and don't be afraid to ask questions.

42

Mary Bowman (Gustafson Porter + Bowman)
→ London, United Kingdom

Cultuurpark Westergasfabriek
Amsterdam, The Netherlands, 1996–2006
At the Cultuurpark Westergasfabriek in Amsterdam, the ground beneath the former gasworks was heavily contaminated. We were required to keep all contaminated ground on site, so by capping it and by creating landforms a landscape with subtle changes in elevation merged seamlessly with the adjacent canal and railway. A series of natural water features provided not only a large lake for bathing but also streams and reed beds, which helped to clean the water.

Architects
Don't Know Everything

As a qualified architect and landscape architect I find it interesting to note a subtle but ever-present assumption that an architect should be the "lead designer" or the "design team lead". At Gustafson Porter + Bowman (GP+B) we have been fortunate enough to lead several large multi-disciplinary teams including architects, engineers and specialists. In this role we can offer a different perspective on space and scale, and apply our knowledge to tie a scheme together and position it in its natural environment. We need to increase understanding of what landscape architects do. We need to share knowledge and work with our clients and other consultants in order to promote the importance of taking care of our public realm. As land-scape architects we are in a unique position to address the challenges of climate change. Architects tend to con-centrate on individual buildings; we need to have a much wider vision of the impact of development on the natural world.

43　Mary Bowman (Gustafson Porter + Bowman)
→ London, United Kingdom

Eiffel Tower site, Paris, France, 2019–ongoing
For the Eiffel Tower project in Paris, GP+B are leading a team of over 20 consultants to create one large park that spans both sides of the Seine. The new buildings being created are enveloped in the landscape. The 54-hectare park will increase the amount of green space by 35% over the existing provision; restrict car traffic; reduce impermeable surfaces; and increase the biodiversity of the existing, picturesque listed gardens.

Embrace
the Unknown

We need to be constantly innovative. Look for a challenge
in all projects, however small or however ambitious. We
can only push the boundaries of our discipline if we constantly seek new ways of approaching the problems and
challenges we face. The construction industries are often
several steps behind the advances in conceptual thinking
and theoretical questioning within our academic institutions. Often though, they hold advances in technical knowledge that can be reinterpreted by the educational and
design disciplines. The dialogue between education, practice and industry should be much more fluid than it tends
to be. Our digital world makes these interconnections
much more possible.

(44) Mary Bowman (Gustafson Porter + Bowman)
→ London, United Kingdom

Diana, Princess of Wales Memorial Fountain,
Hyde Park, London, UK, 2002–2004
This memorial is one of our most memorable projects.
In 2002 digital design was in its infancy. Technology
transfer relocates skills from one industry or discipline
to meet another, completely different set of challenges.
The sinuous stone shapes were digitally designed using techniques borrowed from the car-manufacturing
industry, working with designers more used to modelling vehicle bodies and aircraft parts. The combined
skills of collaborating partners allowed the memorial
to be digitally designed and cut by CNC[1] machines,
something that had not previously been done at this
scale in stone.

1 Computer numerical control milling – a machining
process that employs computerised controls and
rotating, multipoint cutting tools to progressively
remove material from a workpiece, producing custom-
designed components.

Know
your Plants

It is essential to know your plants and understand their role in meeting the environmental and biodiversity challenges we face. Horticultural and arboricultural knowledge is expertise in itself. By collaborating with local experts we gain knowledge of different plant zones. Every epoch has its own approach to planting design, and fashions in planting change with the times. In the 19th century the great plant explorers brought back specimens from all over the world. Today the emphasis is on native planting and our response to climate change. How do we marry a cultural understanding of plants and their origins with a desire to adapt to the native context, which is constantly adjusting with climate change?

45   Mary Bowman (Gustafson Porter + Bowman)
→ London, United Kingdom

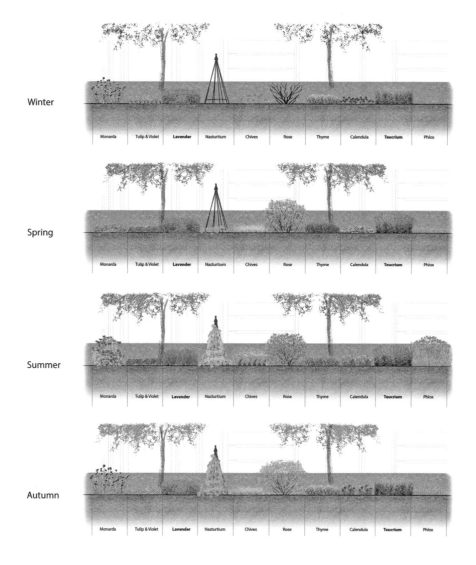

Winter — Monarda | Tulip & Violet | **Lavender** | Nasturtium | Chives | Rose | Thyme | Calendula | **Teucrium** | Phlox

Spring — Monarda | Tulip & Violet | **Lavender** | Nasturtium | Chives | Rose | Thyme | Calendula | **Teucrium** | Phlox

Summer — Monarda | Tulip & Violet | **Lavender** | Nasturtium | Chives | Rose | Thyme | Calendula | **Teucrium** | Phlox

Autumn — Monarda | Tulip & Violet | **Lavender** | Nasturtium | Chives | Rose | Thyme | Calendula | **Teucrium** | Phlox

Mulberry Square, Chelsea Barracks,
London, UK, 2019
The productive garden in Mulberry Square was conceived as a canvas of texture and colour, changing through the seasons. The structure of evergreen lavender and rosemary hedges continues through each of the three zones associated with the kitchen gardens. Organised for seasonal interest, the flowering beds in the southern section create bursts of colour from spring to summer. The herb garden is interplanted with edible flowers, while the productive crops extend the character through winter with retained seed heads and foliage.

Walk

There is nothing immediate or reproducible about land-scape. It must be walked, again and again, through different times, seasons, events. While landscapes lend themselves to photography, painting, poetry, maps and other forms of representation, the only way to truly experience and embrace them is by means of walking. Through movement, one feels gravity, ups and downs, twists and turns, closeness and distance, and the fullness of the landscape medium – from the atmospherics of weather and sky to the topography of contour and place, to the tactility of ground and earth. It is all too easy to think of landscape as image, but it is more fundamentally a medium of journeying, discovery and interaction – a ground of infinite possibility. Aimless wandering, exploring and "taking the path less travelled" can often lead to the most satisfying experiences, even across the most familiar terrain. Get out – and walk!

46 James Corner (Field Operations)
→ New York, NY, USA

Walking along New York's High Line,
New York City, NY, USA
Landscapes and cities can only ever be properly understood through walking, experiencing unfolding scenes
and situations – each bound into the specificity of time,
place and body.

See

While sight might be obvious, seeing is not. To know landscape is to open your eyes to deeper forms of understanding and appreciation. Pay attention to the small things, and open all your senses – looking up, looking down and all around. Behind every surface impression is a much deeper insight; look not only for what is revealed but also for what remains hidden. Feel it, think it, imagine it, see it. See with curiosity, instinct and careful attention, for landscapes contain not only aesthetic and ecological content but also cultural clues: histories, values, ideas. Yes, you see, landscapes are every bit as political and ideological as they are natural, ecological and aesthetic. Seeing is not just about an image impression but more about a deeper understanding of all of the content, meaning and dynamics behind appearances. So, open your eyes – look to see!

47 James Corner (Field Operations)
→ New York, NY, USA

Iceberg
Look below and around the surface of things; see
hidden depths, processes, values, meanings, beauty.

Plot

Landscape architects are plot-makers. They make plans, they stake out and delineate territory, and they unfold the passages of time. Digging, surveying, mapping, planning, founding, shaping, drawing – these are all fundamental activities related to the "emplotment" of land. But plotting speaks more precisely to the alchemy of intent, to the production of content and to the strategic unfolding of events. Certain actions or ingredients placed into play today will most likely precipitate certain effects tomorrow. And because landscapes are so dynamic, bound into ecological time and process, one inevitably catalyses growth and change through how they are shaped, seeded, staged and sustained. Plots have life; plots shape life; and plots instigate life.

48 James Corner (Field Operations)
→ New York, NY, USA

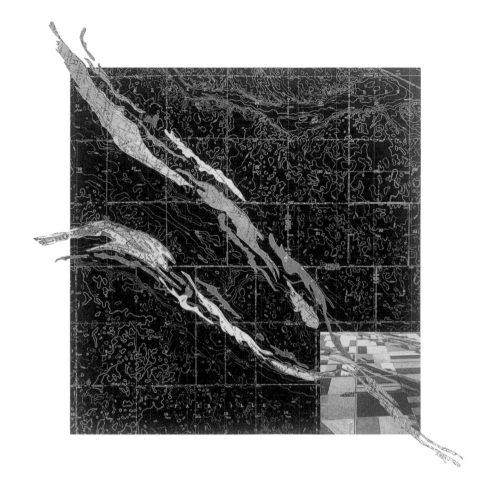

US Survey Grid and Rolling Drifts of Glacial Soil,
collage, James Corner, 1996
Geometrical lines plot out patterns of human occupation, but the vagaries of environmental and local circum-
stance inevitably govern the final form.

Think

Landscape is so closely bound to the earth and to every-day life that it is fundamentally understood as an immediate and practical medium – as a ground to be worked and managed through the skills of the farmer, the gardener, the forester, the surveyor, the ecologist and the like. It is less often understood as a medium for thought, for ideas, for intellectual and cultural innovation. And yet the above three areas all require thinking – critical thinking. Thinking about landscape is key to its own advancement as a cultural milieu. It is also key for any landscape architect trying to communicate the value of landscape to those who don't really understand or care. Thinking allows for more deeply understanding the history of the field, current political and social situations, and the potential for newly relevant future forms of landscape – especially in towns and cities. Thinking broadens what landscape is and what it might still yet become.

49

James Corner (Field Operations)
→ New York, NY, USA

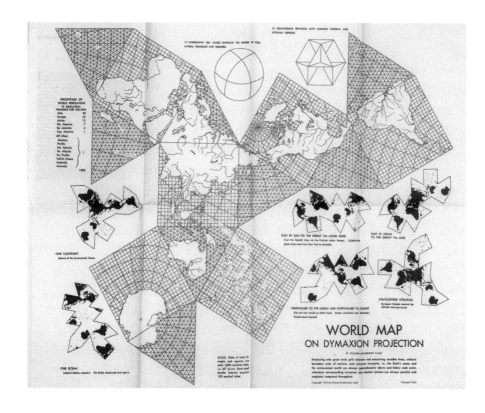

The Dymaxion World Map,
Richard Buckminster Fuller, 1944
The invention of dymaxion projection allowed geography and resources to be unfolded in alternative formats, each prompting thought and conjecture about strategy, relationship and possibility.

Act

Landscapes require a committed, confident, muscular approach toward their shaping. One needs to act boldly, with clarity of intent and a "full-bore" knowledge of the capacity of the medium. A pro-active stance that anticipates needs and potentials is much preferred to a simply reactive approach. Landscape architects should lead, not follow; inaugurate, not patch over. Yet, on the other hand, landscapes are bound so deeply into time, duration, process and change that they are impossible to limit or control. One must instead chart a course and stake out ground while also flexing, adapting and letting certain things go. Landscape is not a handbag or a shoe; it doesn't have the fixity of architecture or the perfection of sculpture; and while it may approximate the time-based choreography of music or film, it is much more promiscuous, wild and eclectic – especially over time. And so, yes: act, and act boldly and with confidence, but also have a healthy stock of humility, restraint and creative adaptability. Act in order to set things in motion, and then be prepared to adapt and change.

(50) James Corner (Field Operations)
→ New York, NY, USA

Flatbed, James Corner, 1996
Devised for an urban planning project in Älvsjö, Stock-
holm, the Flatbed presented a tool for collective thinking,
allowing for various stakeholders to review alternative
maps, plans, programmes and ideas for development.
Through overlay, juxtaposition, scaling and combination,
one thinks through the issues to establish a basis for
action.

Intermediate Natures

We landscape architects believe that the transformation of the landscape is a precedent or a phase in the creation of neighbourhoods. Enhancing a site does not mean prefiguring the road network or city blocks. I like this idea of intermediate nature, of a transformed landscape whose primitive characteristics of spatial orientation, incline and moisture are the preconditions with which town planners and architects will transform the city. I am fascinated by the people who know their land perfectly, who take obvious delight in mastering not only the precise physical reality but also the history and the processes at work. To see, to make legible – this is a necessary precondition but one that cannot take the place of a kind of "interior necessity". The showcasing of traces is not enough. To content oneself with that would be like doing restoration work. But to commandeer these traces, to invert or distort them – therein lies the innovation.

51

Michel Desvigne
→ Paris, France

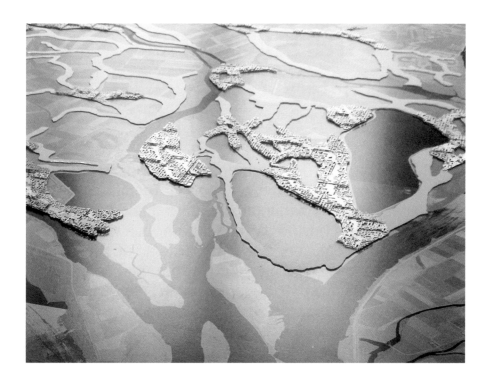

Biesbosch Stad, The Netherlands
The Biesbosch Delta is today an agricultural polder characterised by a fascinating phenomenon of inversion. The cultivated areas of land have sunk due to drainage, while the sand bed of the old creeks has remained at the same level. It is in anticipation of the consequences of climate change that we imagine the delta's transformation by enhancing the geomorphologic process. We propose the construction of a fabric of artificial platforms, on which it will be possible to circulate and live. Landscape architects: Michel Desvigne Paysagiste, 2005

Transforming Landscapes and Shapes of Time

Urban planning and development necessitate long periods of time: periods lasting even longer than the several years necessary for plantings to take root and form. It is crucial to learn how to work and compose with these lengths of time. They can easily become an obstacle – especially if one is intent on executing large urban or landscape compositions that, because of the time involved, either fail to come to fruition or, as a result, are inevitably distorted. But time in this sense of duration can also become an instrument, if clever and artful strategies are conceived and put into place. It requires patience and resistance. This approach advocates for processes. It accepts an economy of means to give sites in transformation an immediate legibility, taking into account present and future developments. It stands firm, makes little design noise and avoids the illusion of premature completion.

52 Michel Desvigne
→ Paris, France

Parc aux Angéliques, Bordeaux, France
This artificial and progressive landscape adapts to the constant transformation of this 75-hectare former industrial site. The project proceeds through a pragmatic approach of substitution: as opportunities arise, each new area acquired by the city is immediately planted.

The very material of the landscape is thus made up of an accumulation of wooded areas and clearings that, as they grow, accommodate new urban uses. The process is successional, and will play itself out over decades. Landscape architects: Michel Desvigne Paysagiste, 2007–ongoing

"Elementary" Writing

I see landscapes as "elementary" compositions. They are made of simple elements – trees, grass, water and paving – whose careful assembly can yield remarkably complex and varied worlds. I like the way our materials defy "outcomes", as if a young landscape could not resemble any model image. Saplings are reminiscent of nothing and yet cover the ground with their dead leaves, immediately transforming the most artificial materials into dusty undergrowth. Paradoxically, simplicity requires innovation and rigour, in the sense of an architecture that is, at the least, visible. This does not entail any theoretical minimalism, but rather the option of rusticity. I like poplar groves, orchards, artificially planted forests. I like to perceive those spaces whose conventional order is forgotten so that they are only variations on density. Neither full nor empty, these squared spaces are sieves of a sort – where, paradoxically, life moves in.

53

Michel Desvigne
→ Paris, France

Otemachi, Tokyo, Japan
Located close to the imperial palace in Tokyo, the new Otemachi Tower and metro station are nestled in a small-scale forest. Pre-grown in the mountains, this forest was transferred tree by tree. This enclave of living materials constitutes a key element within the network of pocket gardens interspersed throughout the neighbourhood. Landscape architects: Michel Desvigne Paysagiste, 2009–2013

Interlocking Scales

Regarding transformation of territories, the most difficult and most important task is to truly see sites, to understand their size and nature, in order to work properly at their various scales. In this matter, we landscape architects are exposed to the same "mistakes" as urban planners when confronted with the difficulty of seeing, understanding, measuring and arbitrating. Comparison with certain scientific works concerning equally complex phenomena shows our fragility and the risk of being satisfied with symbolic, ideological or even commercial approaches to real environmental problems. The physical coherences sought are specific to each scale of intervention, and articulations are necessary for their continuity. The development of a territory cannot expand or contract homothetically. Creating a public space or an urban project at the scale of a neighbourhood differs from intervention on an agglomeration or, moreover, on a large territorial landscape.

54

Michel Desvigne
→ Paris, France

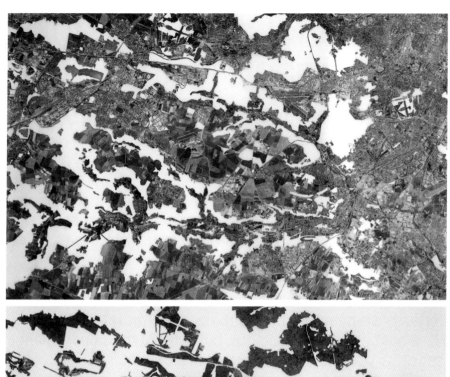

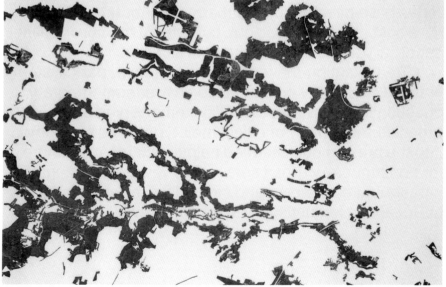

Paris-Saclay, France
The Paris-Saclay urban development plan extends and strengthens a higher education and research site, transforming it into a hub of the future Grand Paris. In order to establish physical cohesiveness without neglecting the different, intermediate levels on which we were working simultaneously, three scales of land-scape intervention had to be defined: the entire territory (7,700 hectares over a distance of 30 kilometres), the urban campus (650 hectares over a distance of 8 kilometres) and the neighbourhoods (200–300 hectares over a distance of 2.5 kilometres). Landscape architects: Michel Desvigne Paysagiste, 2009–ongoing

Frederick Law Olmsted's Legacy: Natural Infrastructure and City Renewal

One of the great singularities of the park systems designed by Olmsted is the way they superimpose themselves on the existing geography, transforming it. From the very beginning of its elaboration, this enhanced geography appeared as a mode of urban development. Contemporary situations differ from those of the 19th century. Industrial zones have developed, and many have mutated. Cities have continued to spread out, but without the public spaces necessary at the scale of these evolutions.

Transplanting the idea of the American park system of the 19th century could help to answer contemporary questions. Just as these park systems served at times to organise the growth of cities, their typology transplanted into the present could indeed help constitute a structure for contemporary urban sprawl. The vestiges of geography, infrastructure networks and industrial sites are the potential locations for just such an urban renewal.

55 Michel Desvigne
→ Paris, France

Euralens, France
The project transforms the vestiges of a vast industrial transport system belonging to an old mining district. Ten kilometres of long wooded bands have been planted as the starting point of a structuring landscape for this area, which has been in crisis for two generations.

What was once considered abandoned, has become the face and place of recovery. In giving the status of landscape to the old routes of the mine, we have also brought about a change in the status of these cities, and of neighbourhoods in the making. Landscape architects: Michel Desvigne Paysagiste, 2010–ongoing

Interplay & Contradiction

Wind, water, heat and cold. In nature, landscape is shaped by the interaction of the elements. When we as designers create landscapes as cultural spaces, it is a conscious act that reflects the interplay of contradictory figurative motifs. Landscape architecture is the culture of sublimated contradictions.

An idea for a landscape emerges in the best cases out of a classical pattern: the interplay of idea and counter-idea, of competing demands, of thesis and antithesis. Built landscape becomes a product of dialectical argumenta-tion. The ongoing confrontation between motif and counter-motif in a design helps overcome preconceived reflexes, often revealing an appropriate response to a specific location.

Good parks are always scenographic constellations in which seemingly contradictory elements produce a stimulating tension. As a stage for urban life, parks must be vibrant but also endlessly hard-wearing and robust for sustained use. At the same time, we expect them to be places of natural tranquility – a habitat, perhaps, for urban lizards.

AW Faust (SINAI)
→ Berlin, Germany

The Concrete Jungle in Frankfurt's Hafenpark embraces contradiction. Its centrally positioned skate park is not solely for the skater scene but is also a vibrant and almost poetic place for everyone.

The City of Frankfurt describes Hafenpark as a park of the 21st century. At four hectares, it is too small to accommodate all the numerous demands voiced in a user survey. As such, extremely contradictory elements adjoin one another: the park is used intensively for sports but also features diverse planting that, along with pockets of meadows, promotes biodiversity.

Mood & Attunement

The "secret" quality of any landscape lies beyond the realm of reason. Alongside what speaks to us on a conscious level, there is always another, silent level of attunement. We describe a landscape's emotional effect as its atmosphere, and when designing we talk about conveying a mood.

We mention this only rarely, however. In the world of engineers, our market expects us to provide a functional, technical service. Instead, we smuggle mood into every project like a trojan horse.

Yet the emotional quality of our surroundings is elementary to urban wellbeing. We need places we can escape to, counterworlds to the barren rationalism of our functional surroundings. As an archetype of designed space, the garden has no explicit purpose – except to move us emotionally.

We have no language with which to express this adequately, only poetry and art. Nevertheless, we continue – consciously or not, explicitly or not – to elaborate and refine the moods of spaces; to assert the place of feelings in a world reigned over by the quantifiable.

57) AW Faust (SINAI)
→ Berlin, Germany

As hard as it is to predict emotions, it is often found or evolved things that move us most. The organic, unplanned and crooked create moments of atmospheric frisson in our man-made surroundings.

When we began working in Bad Lippspringe, the ponds of the Meersmannteiche were clogged with sediment and were barely visible. Today, the woodland ponds are akin to a window in the park – a clearing as distinctive as it is self-evident. Its atmospheric quality, however, owes much to the tall, mature pine trees reflected in the water's surface.

Character & Narration

Places are becoming more interchangeable. As wares, images and styles circulate more widely, many places are losing what gives them character. The quality of design is rising but distinctiveness and emotional attachment are being eroded. Our capacity to identify collectively with these places is waning.

But each place could tell its own unique story – perhaps from its past, maybe a true story, a legend or even wild speculation. Any story can serve as a motif for creating a distinctive sense of place.

The core of such a motif could be the upholding of a local tradition, or a recurring strategic commitment to the regional context. Such concerns suit our slow discipline well. But we can also take this to a new, poetic level, inscribing a free narrative connected with the place into the design to give it a unique, unmistakable quality. In the process, we become storytellers – ideally with a narrative that connects the past with the future.

58   AW Faust (SINAI)
→ Berlin, Germany

Aschersleben is the oldest town in Saxony-Anhalt, and has focused on revitalising its largely depopulated centre. Its historical parks and gardens were renovated for the State Horticulture Show, hosted by the town. A new local park was formed from the remnants of former villa gardens, incorporating the ruins of an orangery – now used by the local primary school – into the public space. The wooden sculpture of an oversized orange by Gisbert Baarmann forms a climbing frame internally and externally, and simultaneously a mnemonic connecting the town's past and future.

Remembrance & Restraint

There are places where history overshadows everything – for example, the sites of Nazi atrocities. Today they are memorials, reminding us in the here and now of crimes past that many would rather not be reminded of. And they are also evidence, bearing witness to those events. Their existence makes it difficult to deny what happened.

Over time many of these places became overgrown and unrecognisable. Woodland grew in Bergen-Belsen and local industry occupied part of Flossenbürg. Since then the lost structures have been made visible once again. They help visitors imagine the past by making it visible in the space of today. Their architectural language is calm, to allow the few remaining authentic testimonies of the past to speak.

In such difficult places, the scope of landscape design is very limited and must be extremely restrained. But it should also create a certain aura that is respectful of the victims and enables their commemoration.

59

AW Faust (SINAI)
→ Berlin, Germany

The shocking footage of British troops liberating Bergen-Belsen made the public aware of the horrific crimes committed at the camp. Some 50,000 people died there, particularly in the final months of the war. In the 1960s a memorial site was created as idyllic heathland on the camp grounds, while woodland sprang up on the rest of the site. The redesign of the site, completed in 2011, concentrated primarily on making the main structures of the camp visible. Corridors and borderlines were cleared in the woodland and marked with a wayfinding system.
Photographer: Klemens Ortmeyer

Economy & Combination

Landscapes learn. They change constantly, always adapting. At present we are witnessing a massive paradigm shift in the urban landscape with climate change, the extinction of species, and boundless land consumption brought on by modern civilisation.

Economy must be our guide. To be sustainable we must contain urban landscapes in order to limit metropolitan expansion. At the same time open spaces must serve ever-more purposes: as fresh-air resources, water reservoirs, noise barriers, havens for endangered species and also as habitats for human use.

The additive repetition of land parcels and functions is no longer tenable. Instead, smart hybrids are emerging that stack functions on top of one another in novel ways.

And we will learn to read the city differently, as the totality of its landscapes and a continuum of its open spaces. Leftover spaces and monofunctional fragments will be no more. Instead, economics will dictate that we maximise the use of every individual square metre.

AW Faust (SINAI)
→ Berlin, Germany

Heilbronn's Neckarbogen formed the backdrop to 2019's Federal Horticultural Show. For the first time this incorporated a new residential quarter, placing renewed focus on the city. Instead of proposing a self-contained park, the project addresses the urban landscape as a system and primarily comprises ribbon-like structures and spaces along the River Neckar and traffic routes. The Hafenberg is a noise barrier on a landfill site, a habitat for lizards, and a lookout plateau with skywalk and picnic areas; the Felsenufer capitalises on its verticality with a climbing wall and vertical playground.

Superman is Boring

The model of a singular heroic lead designer (think: Superman) no longer fits in an increasingly connected and multicultural world. Beyond creating a limited definition of design excellence, the Superman model has enabled some of the least desirable aspects of our profession – namely, practices that lack diversity, are not generous with attribution, and fail to offer work–life balance. Twenty-first-century practice requires new ways of thinking about design process, including notions of coalition building and co-creation. Design process at my practice gives voice and agency to more design contributors, which we know will result in more resonant public spaces that reflect more lived experiences. Great projects are the result of many hands. Embracing and celebrating this will hopefully unleash healthier behaviours – like more creative idea sharing, productive collaboration and good will. Don't these feel essential to the wicked challenges ahead?

61

Gina Ford
→ Cambridge, MA, USA

At Moore Square in Raleigh, North Carolina, I had the pleasure of serving as the lead designer for the Sasaki team, helping to orchestrate an incredible diverse and multidisciplinary team of experts and deep community engagement. The implemented renovation of the Square – thanks, in large part, to the inclusion of many voices – both fits the history and character of its urban context and introduces new and vital uses to a changing downtown district. An urban plaza, shown here, brings together shade, interactive water, movable seating, food outlets, play and restrooms to create a true urban living room.

Focus on the Why

When I told people I was starting my own practice focused on equity and community engagement, a frequent response was something like "You're not doing design anymore?" Design excellence is not mutually exclusive with community engagement. The "what" of design is meaningful, for sure, but the "why" is so much more purposeful for me – particularly for public work, which is so broadly owned. I believe the community is an expert on what is important, what is valuable and what is needed in any given project. Importantly, engagement is fuel for inspired design, not a replacement for it. As a designer, the hard work lies in translating that input – as well as the other layers of the site – into a physical vision. Learn from the site's future users. Be inspired by their needs.

62 Gina Ford
    → Cambridge, MA, USA

To me, the best design enables engagement and connection – places for people to connect with the beauty of a place, with the power of its natural systems and with each other. At the Chicago Riverwalk, I served as the design principal for Sasaki and helped craft spaces that enable both physical connectivity along the river and various gathering places. These spaces serve the needs of residents and visitors alike, allowing an up close and personal connection to the river that didn't exist before.

Be Unafraid to Draw Ugly

Working as an apprentice to waterfront design master Stu Dawson, I learned that there are a million ways to solve one problem. Stu used to ask me to fill a wall with sketches – not as a form of hazing but as training to learn this fact. Too often with clients, team members and students – and especially in the age of computer-based drawing – quick iteration is lost in favour of a single design solution. One of my superpowers as a design leader, I know, is my ability to put ego and perfectionism aside and willingly draw through ideas with a team. Sometimes the best ideas are born out of a series of ugly first passes. Flexibility is important not just to design process but also to project management and construction. Nothing ever goes just the way we plan, so knowing how to adapt quickly and weigh alternative responses is key.

63

Gina Ford
→ Cambridge, MA, USA

SHIFT THE HORIZON

An Enlivened Destination · Connected + Accessible · Cultural Vitality · A Green + Blue Oasis

ECO·VILLAGE

An Enlivened Destination · Connected + Accessible · Cultural Vitality · A Green + Blue Oasis

BRIDGE THE DIVIDE

An Enlivened Destination · Connected + Accessible · Cultural Vitality · A Green + Blue Oasis

I love designing wildly different ideas for a site – giving the client, the community and the design team a diversity of ways of seeing hidden potential. Often rough, fast and gestural, as I did here for layers of design options during the Sarasota Bayfront Master Plan, hand sketching on trace allows for quick iteration, communication and collaboration. The sketches also allow for interpretation, helping me resist the urge to fix or make singular any decisions too early in a process.

Take the Time to Feel

Culture and craft are different everywhere. I work hard to be observant of both – taking in the broader landscape, cultural offerings, food and sites of significance as much as possible when I work in a new place. While we can always rely on local craftspeople and practices to teach us – and we should! – the feel for a place is just as important. I take photographs – lots of photographs – of the wildly beautiful and the profoundly mundane. What I find again and again is that the things that are hardest to photograph – the things that are most fleeting and ephemeral – are often the most useful and essential aspects of a site for design purposes. The climate. The smells. The light. The texture and feel of places. When I can tap into those memories while drawing, I think beautiful things happen. Take the time to feel your site and grab hold of what you learn.

64 Gina Ford
→ Cambridge, MA, USA

Agency's installation – dubbed "XX", as part of the Miller Prize at Exhibit Columbus in Columbus, Indiana – took its inspiration from the elements and stories that had been erased from the given site. A garden of purple flowers recalled plant materials removed from our site.

Grown in movable planters, the flower beds framed changing spaces for gatherings and community happenings focused on surfacing and celebrating the stories of both notable and unsung women in the community.

Make Friends at All Scales

Our profession has the great benefit of operating at multiple scales – from systems thinking and regional planning to detailed design and construction. Landscape architects can "play" with planners and urban strategists as well as architects and engineers. The best work of my career has come from a deep collaborative partnership with another discipline – where multiple ways of seeing a problem bring us to a unique solution. As I launched my own practice, partnering with an urban planner (my business partner Brie Hensold) ensured that the design dialogue would always be rich with ideas and that the broader context would always be present in our work. In partnering with engineers, I continue to learn more efficient and methodical ways of problem solving. I believe it is a gift – not a curse – that our thinking is both as big as a watershed and as small as a joint detail.

65) Gina Ford
→ Cambridge, MA, USA

My work addresses the interaction of natural and cultural systems – weaving together notions of resilience, equity and social cohesion at various scales. This can happen at the regional scale (the White River Vision Plan in Central Indiana, upper left); the site scale (Boulevard Crossing Park in Atlanta, upper right); or the detailed scale (the terraced levee "seatwalls" at Tom Hanafan River's Edge Park, Council Bluffs, lower left); Chicago Riverwalk (lower, right) All of this work relies on deep engagement with systems thinkers like urban planners and focused building experts like engineers.

Unmake, Cultivate the Space!

Cultivating space, making it more spacious,[1] should be considered a seminal act in designing any landscape project. Through unmaking and subtracting we can explore the potential of a new (old) beginning. Unmaking allows us to reclaim ecological values; to unveil hidden layers; and, eventually, to confront the radicality of absence, while speculating about possible futures.

Unmaking is not an *a priori* totalitarian act of completely emptying a site. The deconstruction involved forms part of the design process – as a dialogue between the ethos of the landscape, its ecological processes and its future scenarios. Therefore, "making by unmaking" is not a masterplan; it is an inquiry and a process. This process challenges what the landscape is, while exploring its materiality and dynamics.

66 Martí Franch (Estudi Martí Franch – EMF)
→ Girona, Catalonia, Spain

Club Med restoration project in Cap de Creus
Natural Park, Cadaqués, Catalonia, Spain, 2005–2010
The design brief stipulated the deconstruction of 430
buildings and the ecological restoration of 90 hectares
of coastline. We designed a process of unmaking in
order to reclaim, recycle and rehabilitate the site. Time
was "reversed" to unveil the hidden layers of the landscape's previous inhabitation and to activate its ecological dynamics. During deconstruction work, the rock
outcrops seemed to grow taller and the landscape
expanded as all the attention was channelled towards
the site's basic ingredients: rock, sea and sky. Landscape architects: EMF LA and Ardevols Associates

1   Perejaume, contemporary artist: "…conrear l'espai:
en l'espai de l'espai, podríem dir-ne: en l'espai que
es fa espaiós. Com si hi hagués una llavor de l'extensió"
[Cultivating space, in a space that is made spacious,
as if it contained a seed of extension]. Translation
from Catalan by Martí Franch, from Perejaume (2015).
Paraules locals. Sant Celoni: Tushita Edicions, p. 49.

Design by Management

Tailor an open mode of practice that plays with ecological succession.

Landscapes – fields, meadows, forests and so on – are a result of the tension between the regimes of care – ploughing, sowing, grazing, mowing, cutting – and the regimes of neglect and ecological succession. The evolution of the vast majority of landscapes can be regulated through a very limited number of low-tech, low-cost interventions. Therefore, the frequency of management activities dictates a landscape's stage in the sequence of ecological succession.

Since Gilles Clément's seminal work about *differentiated management* with his "Garden in Motion" concept, this practice has developed into a powerful tool to incorporate spatial, experiential and ecological intelligence into landscape management. Through the choreography of its regimes of care, *design by differentiated management* facilitates ecological diversification; citizen appropriation; and, ultimately, the exploration of new forms of beauty.

67) Martí Franch (Estudi Martí Franch – EMF)
→ Girona, Catalonia, Spain

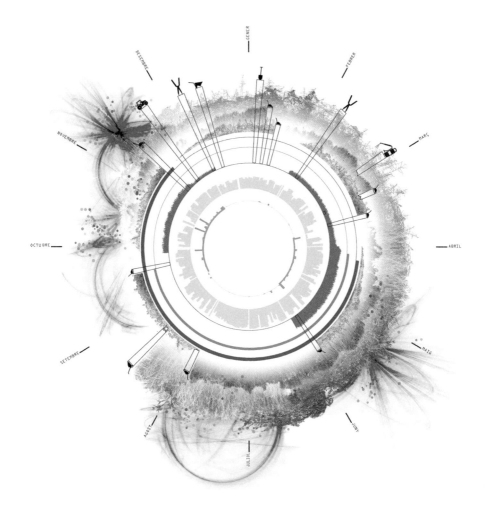

The Shore project, Girona, Catalonia, Spain, 2014–ongoing

"Girona-shores" is a self-initiated research project that has developed into an ongoing public commission. It aims to foster the establishment of a "green" infrastructure network in Girona by implementing creative management tactics and connecting together the naturban spaces surrounding the town – its "shores". As a result of a specifically designed regime of care, an abundant land mosaic emerges that enhances biodiversity and can be apprehended and appropriated by the town's citizens. This *Design by Management* praxis has the capacity to adapt continuously to evolving conditions. Landscape architects: EMF LA

Multiply the Shore!

Water is the origin of life and an essential element for any biome. The biome's "shore", the ecotone where land and water meet and integrate, is the most desired life strip for humans and animals alike. Many different forms of life depend on, compete over and have adapted to be able to thrive in this land–water zone.

Moulding the shore – playing with its cross-section, edge conditions, materiality, topography and width – creates opportunities to multiply the biodiversity and the experiential quality of a space. The design of the shore triggers a chain of ecological processes that self-regulate through natural succession.

If we "consider nature as an ally and not as a guest",[1] and accept that "we are just creating the departing conditions on which the landscape generates its own advent, then, in this shared action, the work of the landscape architect finds its sustainability".[2]

68 Martí Franch (Estudi Martí Franch – EMF)
→ Girona, Catalonia, Spain

"Parco dalla Pace", Vicenza, Italy, 2015–2022
In the terrain of Vicenza's former airport, the water table lies 70 to 100 centimetres below the fertile soil. The "skeleton" of the new park is made by excavating and modelling the existing soil in search of ground water. As a result of this basic and inexpensive process, an extremely varied "blue" mosaic emerges – with very diverse edge conditions, shores and habitats ready to be explored and appropriated. The park, currently under construction, is already bursting with life. PAN Associ-ates + EMF LA + Zagari + Asprostudio + ITS + M Díaz

1   Geoffroy-Dechaume, Guillaume (2006). *Le Parc du Chemin de l'Île, une étape de la promenade bleue.* Nanterre: Conseil général des Hauts-de-Seine, p. 23.

2   Michel Corajoud, from the essay "To the students of the schools of landscape-architecture [sic]", 2000. http://corajoudmichel.nerim.net/10-textes/elements-des-9-conduites/10neuf-conduites-traduction.htm (accessed 18.02.2021).

Siting a Path as if only the Feet Could See

Siting a path is the seminal act of unfolding and reading a landscape. To do this, escape the studio, go on site and use your feet to map the paths that open up like you use a pencil to draw a sketch. Activating all senses, an experiential cartography of the site's riches emerges – saturated with the nuances of light, smells, sounds, sights and anecdotes. Site visits transform into a precious body of knowledge about materiality, light, effort, visual surprises, vertigo and so on.

Back in the studio, these "foot sketches" are woven into the design speculation for the project. When construction begins, each decision ought to be renegotiated metre by metre in order to adapt to its changing conditions – so that, in fact, most decisions are made on site and during the execution of the project.

69

Martí Franch (Estudi Martí Franch – EMF)
→ Girona, Catalonia, Spain

Catalan coastal walks: Cap de Creus, Spain,
2010 (above); Palamós, Spain, 2021 (below)
These two coastal walks negotiate materiality and footprint with the existing rock outcrops. Landscape architects: EMF LA and Ardévols Associates

Know When to Throw Confetti

Daily routines, Hannah Arendt once provocatively observed, leave little trace in consciousness; ...ordinary experience doesn't much register if it lacks disruptive drama.[1] Richard Sennett

Drama, celebration, surprise and astonishment ought thus to be a critical part of a project if it aims to register in the visitor's memory.

"Ad hoc" designed artefacts, actions or events – called confetti – create disruptive experiential moments, slow the visitors' pace and invite them to view the landscape with new eyes.[2] This is the challenge: to find the precise spot and to design an intervention capable of offering a new landscape reading and appreciation.

Such "confetti" aren't architectural follies; they do not impose design gestures, abstracted narratives or intellectual quotes – they are discreet and austere celebrations that aim to direct the visitors' attention to the beauty of the landscape. It takes multiple walks to discover the right spot, and it requires time to design the disruptive interfaces needed to celebrate the peculiar. Therefore, confetti comprise new signs conceived to act as catalysts of wonder; affection; and, ultimately, care while unveiling new readings.

70

Martí Franch (Estudi Martí Franch – EMF)
→ Girona, Catalonia, Spain

The Shore green infrastructure project,
Girona, Catalonia, Spain, 2014–ongoing
The use of "confetti" to create an eloquent place: cutting geometrical paths into the prairie, lenses to discover nummulite fossils, graphics on pacified streets or "ad hoc" furniture to stimulate discovery and appropriation. Further examples of such confetti include heritage and rock clearance, picnic spots and chill-out *tatamis* with views, vantage points etc. Landscape architects: EMF LA & Girona Municipality

1 Richard Sennett on "The Public Realm". https://intensificantvidesnervioses.files. wordpress.com/2013/08/the-public-realm_-sennett. pdf (accessed 18.02.2021).

2 "The real voyage of discovery consists not in seeking new landscapes, but in having new eyes". http://www.age-of-the-sage.org/quotations/proust_ having_seeing_with_new_eyes.html (accessed 08.05.2021).

To be an Engineer…

Landscape architecture, from our point of view, always starts within the logic of engineering. The physical reality of the soil and water cannot be forgotten or ignored – it is the starting point of design thinking. This ideology is anchored, more or less, in a systemic approach. Without this, landscape architecture becomes impossible – we are all a part of the planet, we all exist within a climate, we are all a part of an ecosystem.

   The ecosystem is very complex, with many layers and biotopes. Springtime splendour can only exist if you understand the midwinter condition. I believe landscape architects should know the logic of life science and engineering – to understand the planet, working from its geology, soil and ecology.

71 Adriaan Geuze (West 8)
→ Rotterdam, The Netherlands

The Grand Egyptian Museum,
Giza, Egypt, 2004–2012
The relationship between the plateau and the pyramids.
West 8 joined the winning architectural team to refine the concept of the museum, to prepare a design for the garden and to develop a masterplan for the museum's environment in relation to the Pyramids of Giza.
Landscape architects: West 8

...and to be a Poet

Landscape architecture is born from a spirit and, simultaneously, a sense of place. This is where the "architecture" in "landscape architecture" is particularly relevant: it relates to the study and creation of identity, illusions and narrative. Equally, we are not "landscape engineers" – we don't simply do *calculations* – our profession is for me, in a word, poetry.

Landscape architects should know how to sculpt; they are working from a legacy of the past, there is relevance in the continuity of history. Land is inherited: it is gifted from several previous generations and then passed on to new ones. Each generation adds a level, a layer of the sublime, a debate, a smile, a polemic, a position, an experiment – but, without a doubt, land is part of the cultural realm and therefore becomes part of the cultural reality.

(72) Adriaan Geuze (West 8)
→ Rotterdam, The Netherlands

Máximapark Pergola, Leidsche Rijn,
The Netherlands, 1997–ongoing
A system of individual and interchangeable precast
elements coated in a cloak of ivy. The pergola functions as a veil drawn around the "Binnenhof" courtyard, enabling the core of this design to be perceived

as an illusion of paradise. Infrastructure-like in scale,
the pergola towers 6 metres above the ground and
spans over a length of 3.5 kilometres. Its honeycomb-
like cells are fitted with custom-made bat boxes, in-
sect hotels and planters. Landscape architects: West 8

Freedom

Evolution has allowed us to adapt to any context – and that, for me, is very relevant for connectivity. If humans, people, citizens use a public space, use the landscape, they desire the freedom to adapt to it.

A dominant portion of our world has become 100% functional: everything in it is preoccupied with a dedicated intention. We are bombarded with commercial illusions and the banalities of capitalism – cameras, security, algorithms manipulate how we explore and "read" the world. Landscape architecture should deliver spaces that are not pre-occupied but that prioritise self-reflection and perception. We should detoxify the public realm – bring back the antidote: space for people to feel and be themselves.

Give people a sense of freedom to navigate their own world and reality. I notice this makes people happy – euphoric, even. We are children; we want to play and fool around and take directions from our own brains.

73 Adriaan Geuze (West 8)
→ Rotterdam, The Netherlands

RE-USED SEAWALL GRANITE

The "Scramble" on Governors Island, New York City, NY, USA, 2007–2016
The "Scramble" on Outlook Hill, one of the four man-made hills on Governors Island, is made with reclaimed granite blocks from the island's former sea wall. It is an expression of the adaptability and materiality reuse that forms part of Governors Island's "DNA". Landscape architects: West 8

Growth

For me, landscape architecture is a specific attitude and discipline – different from design. Landscape architects "read" the world as a controlled constellation, and have a second nature that understands and deeply embodies the notion of progressive development across generations.

Landscape architecture fundamentally forms part of a system of thinking in which growth, evolution and transformation are the paradigm. All landscape architects, whatever their training, understand seasonality and plant life – growth and change. From this unique mindset, arising from their education, they are therefore easily capable of understanding a slow-moving, but ever-changing, world. Landscape architects should think in terms of nonpermanent reality since reality is, in fact, in motion, in transition, is fluid.

No doubt the best we can do is plant good, young material and hope for the right seasons to come and bring it to fruition. Good landscape architecture is deeply embodied, rooted and anchored in the logic of Mother Nature.

74 Adriaan Geuze (West 8)
→ Rotterdam, The Netherlands

Markeroog, Markermeer, The Netherlands, 2006
A masterplan for a big city to be born within a swamp, the Markeroog was a plan to combine the cleaning and ecological restoration of the IJmeer and Marker-meer with residential development. A new connective city, northeast of Amsterdam, born within a swamp. Landscape architects: West 8

The Lonely Hearted

As a profession practising in the realm of contemporary mass culture, landscape architecture is expected to cultivate a perfect picture of innocence: eternal spring, children's balloons, flapping butterflies, cherry blossom, peace and harmony.

However, landscape architects don't design the innocent. We should design a space as it will be, not just bathed in sunlight but also at the dead of night. The imagery of landscape architecture is often more radical than it is "Disney"!

Strangely enough, we should not forget that most of us are lonely-hearted; we are full of desires and melancholy. Lonely-hearted people relate to midwinter, the wind of the autumn, the snow in the park, the midnight silence of the street, the moonlight in the garden. It is not always the drama, it is the still life. It is about consolation, solace and mercy.

(75) Adriaan Geuze (West 8)
→ Rotterdam, The Netherlands

Schouwburgplein, Rotterdam, The Netherlands, 1991–1996
Design in the rain. The square creates a stage for its inhabitants to become the performers, illuminated by crane-like hydraulic lamps. The design of Schouwburg-plein, or "Theater Square", was generated entirely from its situation in the heart of Rotterdam. By its particular framing of space, it shows the value of the unpro-grammed void–a space that invites spontaneous activ-ity. Landscape architects: West 8

Soil Biodiversity is Critical Infrastructure

Soils are sensual. They have texture, scent, colour. They are the living skin of the planet, with more microbes in a handful than people on the Earth. Grab one, lift it to your nose. With your eyes closed detect its health and read a living dynamic – physically, chemically and biologically complex – that is the foundation of all life. Observe how the material rolls between your fingers as a cohesive or a crumbling joint. Register the moisture and granularity. Look for white, stringy signs of fungal hyphae and earthworm activity. Every trial pit illuminates a profile of great substance. Humus, topsoil, subsoil and even parent material that reveal the characteristics of the resource, alive with a below-ground narrative of physical and human geography. Soil is critical infrastructure on which our very existence relies. The geological layer cake beneath our feet encapsulates our fundamental identity in an illustration of deep time and human endeavour.

76

Johanna Gibbons
→ London, United Kingdom

Soil Vitrine

Designed by Johanna Gibbons in collaboration with soil scientist Tim O'Hare, the vitrine highlights the beauty of natural and anthropogenic soil profiles hidden in the congested below ground world of the city. Each glass vial reveals a different typical profile – city parkland, industrial, anthropogenic, tree-rooting substrate beneath pavement and tree-rooting zone in open soil – that provides for urban nature. The installation reveals structural complexities and colour coding of manufactured and natural soil profiles, flecked with fragments of human activity.

The Urban Forest Bridges the Gap between Humanity and the Natural World

Urban forests are complex, diverse and enchanting eco-systems connecting time and territory over the centuries. They are structurally astounding, being shaped by climatic, atmospheric, anthropogenic and geological influences, anchoring the ground and holding open the soil. They provide an extraordinary range of resources, clean air, biodiversity, cooling and carbon sequestration. The urban forest underpins health and wellbeing in the city, including the cumulative and beneficial slow-release effects on mental resilience as a result of being in contact with nature. Being drenched in woodland beauty can be life enhancing. The shadow play in early spring, the sculptural qualities of standing deadwood hosting a world of microhabitats, or the softness of layers of sweet-smelling earthy aromas underfoot, bring microbial life to the engineered environment. The urban forest is an essential part of the character and heritage of the city, creating deep emotional bonds between the life force of the forest and our own.

(77) Johanna Gibbons
→ London, United Kingdom

Garden House Ghost Sign London, UK
Far from being an inert technology, the urban forest is a natural, refined and responsive system enabling our evolutionary adjustment to city dwelling. Designed by Pentagram, the "PLANT TREES" ghost sign was commissioned by Johanna Gibbons to "speak" to the street. It sits high on an endterrace blind window, while the garden itself assists biodiversity and urban bee pollination. An aerial hedge of crab apples, flowering profusely in early spring with jewel-like fruit, and fastigiate white willows, irrigated by disconnected downpipes, create an elegant, dynamic and diaphanous cushion to city living.

Sustaining Life is a Prerequisite of Design Excellence

The landscape,
the soil
that lies below,
the archaeology that tells us where we came from,
veteran trees
that connect the skies with the earth,
that cool and cleanse the air,
a canopy, broad and full of life, under which we shelter,
which envelopes our streets with beauty,
breathes life, signals the seasons,
without which there would be no birdsong.
A life cycle at the intersection of
geology, biodiversity, architecture, social history.

The city is a dynamic landscape,
with an ambiguous wildness
that can bring us close
to nature and natural process.
It is this landscape that connects us all,
within which, for a moment in geological time
the landscape architect plays a part,
conserving while curating
a delicate balance of the ecosystem,
natural and unnatural beauty,
complexities embraced with quiet conviction,
the task
to sustain life and create places
that can be loved.

78

Johanna Gibbons
→ London, United Kingdom

Inger Munch's Pier, Oslo, Norway

Inger Munch's Pier is a collaboration between British artist Tracey Emin and J&L Gibbons. The Mother is a 9-metre-high bronze, kneeling, naked to the elements and visible from across the harbour. The concept for the pier is to make porous and absorbent the engineered structure, to contour a coastal ecology with graded growing media, in the midst of an ecological desert. This "seed bed" will evolve as a dynamic microhabitat supporting urban bee pollination and coastal birdlife in the heart of the city; an unexpected urban meadow within which The Mother is brought to earth.

Innovation Happens on the Margins of Collaborative Practice

Life in practice is constantly shifting to ride evitable change, to fine tune the way we can contribute most effectively in the field we love and to which my practice feels a deep responsibility. J&L Gibbons does not seek to grow in size but rather in influence through collaborations and conversations with colleagues, clients and communities whom we work with, envisioning landscapes that bind our lives together in a way that is meaningful and relevant. My interest is in nurturing long-term collaborations, to re-envisage landscapes carried out with scientific rigour, through active engagement. Whether alongside soil scientist Tim O'Hare or in the wandering discourse with our poet-in-residence, S. J. Fowler, ideas are cross-fertilised. A vigorous exploration of where design ingenuity and purpose lie, defining technical, cultural and philosophical relationships, that always goes far beyond what we are asked to do.

79

Johanna Gibbons
→ London, United Kingdom

Landscape Learn – Winter Dormancy
Hosted by Phytology London, UK
Landscape Learn is our social enterprise. It uses the seasonality of nature to structure an alternative approach to adaptive, cross-disciplinary and immersive practice and research. It is open to students, professionals and communities, and is hosted by a network of landscape experts providing an agile, process-driven and collaborative method of sharing knowledge and experience to stimulate innovative thinking. I believe it is at the margins of the arts and sciences that a delicate, fascinating and complex weave of heritage, ecology, design, art, engineering and care taking can be transformative.

Stewardship Grows from Community Empowerment

As designers, it is in our nature to look and listen closely while acting strategically. Now set within the context of interconnected global emergencies – biodiversity, health and climate change – it is vital that local action nurture community capacity alongside ecological resilience. The potential is there to affect visceral engagement in post-industrial landscapes, all too often disregarded as a messy mosaic of anthropogenic intervention and ruderal ecology. To revel in ambiguities of nature and human nature, debunking preconceptions of what is natural, as today, no habitat remains unaltered by humanity. The imperative is to address the dynamics of change, community cohesion and landscape restoration and the subtle aesthetics of a city's "natural" world, and to envisage landscapes through a process-driven approach. This calls for a generous philosophy of openness that stimulates strong political backing and empowers the local community by investing in stewardship skills to underpin long-term sustainability.

(80) Johanna Gibbons
→ London, United Kingdom

Dalston Eastern Curve Garden, London, UK
J&L Gibbons with muf architecture/art pioneered a multifaceted creative process of engagement, design and governance with an eco-centric approach. It sought to realise how diverse facets of the community could be part of a concept of ecological patchiness; how intricate forms of urban wildness could persuasively insinuate a new form of healthy and civilised society. It is "radical, eccentric and people based",[1] self-sustaining by the local community who shared time together with us, in a continual feedback loop of in-situ action research and design exploration.

1   Ken Worpole: https://thenewenglishlandscape. wordpress.com/2017/04/14/insurgent-gardens-the-dalston-eastern-curve-garden/ (accessed 08.05.2021).

How to Foster the Feeling of Community and Togetherness

A park should bring people together. It should give rise to a feeling of social closeness and a shared identity. Creating a relaxed atmosphere can contribute towards mitigating social tensions, or not even allowing them to arise in the first place. To achieve this, it is necessary on the one hand to encourage communication in a targeted manner, and on the other to produce a feeling of togetherness. How can this be realised using the means of landscape architecture?

The "stages and stands" principle stages the coming together of people who would otherwise never take note of each other. Many people want to do things in a park: to enjoy life and show off, to let others share in their abilities and hobbies. For this to work, there needs to be someone who does something and someone who watches – and perhaps even marvels. This results in interaction and communication.

81 Leonard Grosch (LOIDL)
→ Berlin, Germany

Apart from the idea of stages and stands – like the big stage here in Berlin's Park am Gleisdreieck – other concepts, such as positioning various "offerings" very close to and in reference to one another, can create an atmosphere of community. People have the impression of being together without really doing anything together. This is supposed to give people a feeling of a shared identity; integration; and peaceful, harmonious togetherness.

About the Importance of the Framework of a Park

A strong framework ensures the superordinate spatial qualities and the functional and staging connections required of a park in the long run – even if the contents of individual spaces change over the course of time. It makes possible the holding together of different atmospheres and aesthetics spatially, functionally and in terms of design. In the future, the co-determination and joint designing of parks and its diverse desires and demands will only further gain in importance. This makes robust park structures that much more important.

So what does "framework" mean? A park framework is comparable to the structural design of a building: it is composed of the spatial framework, the network of paths, the structuring of the areas that arise and the most important structuring – and, generally, also staging – that of installations.

The components of this framework determine one another. When designing, it is possible to verify the framework through successively withdrawing structure-giving components: at what point does the spatial and functional cohesion disintegrate?

82 Leonard Grosch (LOIDL)
→ Berlin, Germany

In the case of Park am Gleisdreieck, the space and structure are oriented toward what was found on the site: the superordinate spatial framework comprises a plateau with two clearings that is elevated above the urban space and framed by trees. Its quality lies in the simplicity of the configuration: the succinct contrast between vastness and density. This clear arrangement is also functionally efficient: it facilitates the integration of all intensive uses into the framework, and thus keeps the centre of the park open.

How to Create Multicoded Objects

It should be possible not only to use the elements of a park in an outstanding way; in an ideal case, they should also inspire creative use and unforeseen activities. For this reason, for me, a park should also include elements that do not have a clearly recognisable use and that offer so much sophistication that they prompt people to appropriate or use them in unexpected ways. Such open-ended objects and installations, along with areas with specific purposes, should be so stimulating in form and material that people want to touch them or climb on them – or desire to use them in some way. In other words, they should make people want to appropriate them. The hope, so to speak, is that this animation is able to address a majority of users. It is specifically indeterminacy with respect to use that entices.

83) Leonard Grosch (LOIDL)
→ Berlin, Germany

The topography of springy green EPDM rubber and hard asphalt models the area in an alternation between low elevations and raised flat surfaces. This results in the creation of a range of smaller spaces using one means of design. As planners, we anticipate that particular uses will take place at particular locations without being able to specify the whole spectrum of actions in advance. The more unforeseen uses and activities that take place, the more pleased I am. For me, a range of uses in one place is proof of the landscape elements' ability to animate a space.

Wildness is Important in the City

Wildness is important in a city, and should be a basic component of its parks. And not only that: apart from their ecological functions, different forms of vegetation should reflect the variety of city dwellers' needs and desires for wild nature. These needs can be of a purely contemplative or atmospheric sort, or be expressed as a desire to participate – for instance, through gardening together. The contrast between wild and designed forms of vegetation makes both seem more valuable.

As far as dealing with vegetation is concerned, my view of parks was also honed and altered during the planning process for Berlin's Park am Gleisdreieck. In the meantime, I find that it is not possible to appreciate wild vegetation highly enough.

Where there is ruderal vegetation, it transmits similar qualities to its wild counterpart in the form of the patina on structural relicts. In impression, wild vegetation often displays a more complex quality than designed planting. If park sites do not offer any wild vegetation, I would in most cases advise establishing wild areas or allowing existing areas to run wild.

(84) Leonard Grosch (LOIDL)
→ Berlin, Germany

One can either save existing areas of wilderness or create new ones. At Park am Gleisdreieck, we did both – saving the areas of the former freight yard, which had become overgrown over decades, and those where borders of robinia, birches, trees of heaven, poplars, oleasters and oaks had formed. In addition to these existing wild areas, we planted numerous new flower meadows – from shade and sage meadows to dry grasslands.

There Always Has to be Effective Contrast

I cannot emphasise strongly enough how important contrast is in a design. I think a design always needs well-set, effective contrasts to make it interesting, stimulating and lively. The one I love most is the contrast produced by wild nature as a backdrop for highly artificial places and objects – or the contrast between rich wilderness and generous, large, simple surfaces. Places that have been informally assembled by citizens themselves contrast very effectively with artificial architectonic scenes. The contrast between levelled-out, flat lawn and high, diverse meadow is a traditional theme in the landscape gardens of the Romantic era, which still have a timelessly strong effect and validity. To be aware of and precise in using different types of contrast is also a very useful tool in order to achieve a "readable" park design, because the particular design elements are distinguished from each other naturally.

85

Leonard Grosch (LOIDL)
→ Berlin, Germany

In the Baakenpark in Hamburg, artificial play areas contrast with wildflower meadows. The meadow, with its complex textures, atmospherically enriches the slick surface of the grey EPDM rubber. On the upper level, a soccer field made from artificial lawn contrasts in the same way with the surrounding wild meadows. What you cannot see here is that the entire park, with its dramatic topography, contrasts as a whole with the often calm water of the adjoining River Elbe.

Landscapes are Palimpsests

Beneath the surface landscapes are layered sectionally with the detritus of time. Whether built material or organic, these layers are the artefacts of life. They reveal to us how previous inhabitants shaped and organised their world. These layers also reference ecological change – whether passively evolutionary or cataclysmic. Together they combine to create an ecological history, revealing to us that landscapes – and, particularly, sites – are never empty. So when we design, we must be careful of what we exhume or what we cover up.

86

Walter Hood
→ Oakland, CA, USA

Front Yard, Rosa Parks Neighborhood, Detroit, MI, USA

Landscape is a Medium

The landscape communicates and expresses a society's beliefs and meanings, indicating how it defines itself and others in the world. Landscape comprises physical and visual components that together form a specific spatial and environmental logic. The medium is used to express both privilege and power, and subservience and value. It also expresses a society's value and belief in what is beautiful and meaningful. If it is not considered in this multidimensional and complex manner, the medium is rendered exclusive and unrepresentative of the society's citizenry. The medium composed is a proscenium for the world in which we live.

(87) Walter Hood
→ Oakland, CA, USA

View of planted tree *allée*, Florence, Italy

Landscapes Tell Stories Whether We Write Them or Not

Landscapes are rhetorical. Our stories are comparative, mythical, pedagogical… structured as similes, allegories, analogies and metaphors. Most landscapes tell the story of their current origins; we just have to look closely at the manner in which they are constructed, spatialised and occupied. In the USA, the open-lot plan recounts the story of colonisation and democracy as compared with a medieval town in Italy, which tells the story of accretion and time. The unbuilt landscape can tell the story of succession and change, or of climate and evolution.

88 Walter Hood
→ Oakland, CA, USA

Altar in the garden, San Carlos Borromeo de Carmelo
Mission, Carmel, CA, USA

Landscapes are Entropic

Landscapes want to be messy. Landscapes are in a constant stage of becoming... uncertainty and disorder are innate to their sensibility. Human environments are ordered and certain, holding back landscapes in order to be clean and definable. We have to find opportunities to engage with this process as we design and construct our cities and neighbourhoods, so that landscape evolves rather than being maintained in a constant state. This challenges the current reactionary stance towards change – as we see with climate change – and suggests that we embrace the Earth's flux.

(89) Walter Hood
→ Oakland, CA, USA

Aerial view of Massapequa, Long Island, NY, USA

Landscapes are Political and Contested Spaces

Humans, like other animals, are territorial. Spaces and landscapes have been colonised throughout history, creating the context for contestation and the politics of the state. Even as spaces are decolonised, the residues of their structures are still present in built typologies that remain valued and maintained. Many spaces are civic landscapes, which in most societies are public; streets, plazas/squares and even parks bear this legacy, and continue to be shaped by political and social change.

90

Walter Hood
→ Oakland, CA, USA

Free Speech Monument – "60,000 Feet Tall" – Sproul
Plaza, University of California Berkeley, Berkeley, CA,
USA

Ingenious Loci

For generations the code of conduct of the landscape profession was embodied in the concept of consulting the *genius loci*, originally popularised by Alexander Pope as "genius of the place". But what about the landscape without qualities? What to consult when there is no "there" there? How to make the ordinary into the extraordinary? Genius implies an exceptional capacity for imaginative creation, original thought, curiosity, invention and discovery. As landscape architects, we should rattle the cage of the *genius loci*. But beware the false prophets of authenticity. Let's replace singular views with a multitude of different visions. Landscape architecture interacts in a complex continuum with humankind and nature, town and country, land and architecture. We no longer reconcile the duality of opposite forces but orchestrate and choreograph a multitude of dynamic and hybrid interactions. The old is dying and the new is not yet born. We need genius on steroids; we need to consult our very own Ingenious Loci.

91

Eelco Hooftman (GROSS. MAX)
→ Edinburgh, United Kingdom

Indoor/outdoor swimming pool

Learning from Ascension Island: Darwin, Hooker and the Art of Nature Activation

Instead of static Nature Conservation (the kiss of death in times of climate change) we should promote dynamic Nature Activation. An early experiment on the remote Ascension Island acts as an inspiration that entire eco-systems can be created from scratch. Charles Darwin visited the island in 1836 as part of his five-year scientific expedition on the Beagle. At the time of Darwin's visit, the island was devoid of vegetation, and a lack of fresh water prohibited its strategic use. Darwin, with a little help from Joseph Hooker of Kew Gardens, devised a cunning plan to arrange for shipments of plants from Africa, South America and even from Kew itself to create a cloud forest on the island's extinct volcano. This man-made piece of hyper-nature started to gather sea mist, and rainfall was collected in a specially constructed dew pond. Ingenious loci avant la lettre! We used this example as inspiration for our concept of the "Ecological Wonderbra", patented as an uplifting support system for fragile eco-systems.

92

Eelco Hooftman (GROSS. MAX)
→ Edinburgh, United Kingdom

Charles Darwin – naturalist and architect
of hyper-nature

To Think is to Speculate with Images

Landscape can present a world in several dimensions at once. A viewpoint represents also a point of view. The Scottish Enlightenment philosopher David Hume observed that "the mind is a kind of theatre, where several perceptions successively make their appearances; pass, re-pass, glide away and mingle in an infinite variety of postures and situations".[1] Indeed, a myriad of images stir our imagination. Landscape is a visual discipline that originates from the world of painting. Sometimes we long for those days when landscape was to be considered not just important – but the most important branch of aesthetics. The Picturesque opened our eyes for a dynamic succession of painterly pictures based upon multiple viewpoints assuming movement. Nowadays, the pixel is our pigment, the screen our canvas. Once we were interviewed to design the landscape for the new European headquarters of Goldman Sachs in London. A double-breasted stockbroker asked us to explain what we do in one sentence. Our answer was direct and simple: you speculate with money, we speculate with images.

(93) Eelco Hooftman (GROSS. MAX)
→ Edinburgh, United Kingdom

Vertical garden

1   Hume, David (1985; first published 1739).
A Treatise of Human Nature. London: Penguin Classics,
p. 301.

Romantic Agony

Landscape architects, wild at heart, are the last of the romantics. Maybe it is the nature of our medium, which is all about the passage of time – about growth and decay, beauty and the sublime. Maybe it is our longing for Paradise Lost. Landscapes can be read as palimpsests of narratives, each generation scratching the surface to inscribe their mark. There is no beginning and no end, only an endless state of becoming. Perfect beauty resides only in a fragmentary and temporary state. The emotive wilderness of the landscape architect is our inner strength. Landscape architects are the natural successors of architects and urbanists to transform our post-pandemic cities. In *Observations sur l'architecture* (1765), Laugier wrote, "Whoever knows how to design a park well will have no difficulty in tracing the plan for the building of a city […]. There must be regularity and fantasy, relationships and oppositions, and casual, unexpected elements that vary the scene; great order in the details, confusion, uproar, and tumult in the whole."[1]

94

Eelco Hooftman (GROSS. MAX)
→ Edinburgh, United Kingdom

1   Laugier, Marc Antoine (1765). *Observations sur L'Architecture*, quoted in Bernard Tschumi (1990). "The Pleasure of Architecture", *Questions of Space*, chapter 10. London: Architectural Association, p. 50.

2   Breton, André (1992; first published 1929). "Premiere exposition Dali", *Oeuvres Completes 11*. Paris: Gallimard, pp. 307–309.

Everything depends on our deliberate hallucinations. [2]
André Breton

We are the Children of the Google Earth Revolution

Once upon a time landscape architecture was defined according to strict and well-guarded geographic borders. The Dutch kept relentlessly draining their eternal swamp, proclaiming their national mantra that "God created the world but the Dutch created the Netherlands". In Denmark, angry young landscape architects sharpened their pencils and, by a stretch of the imagination, caused a revolution of sorts by changing the oval into an ellipse. The Germans – regardless of fascist or communist inclination – fanatically idolised a hardcore "body and soil" ecology as a united nationalist ideology. The French groped among the dry bones of their past. Meanwhile, the making of the British landscape remained the preserve of dabbling, babbling upper-class dilettantes under the governance of their very own "Ministry of Silly Walks". All this has dramatically changed. We now operate in an age characterised by the dissolution of boundaries. Landscape has become a melting pot of globalised cultures. We work around the clock in all different time zones. We have jumped the fence and see the whole world as our garden. We are, indeed, the Children of the Google Earth Revolution.

95 Eelco Hooftman (GROSS. MAX)
→ Edinburgh, United Kingdom

Garden for a plant collector, China

Land Agreements

Landscape architecture projects start with a property
survey, a land title, a boundary line. These are taken as legal
fact, as professional authority. But how did that line get
drawn, how did that landscape first become a property
and what does that have to do with a contemporary design
project? If you're in Canada or the United States, what
treaties or agreements were signed between Indigenous
nations and the British Crown or federal governments
in this place, and how have they been honoured or dishonoured since? Who is currently fighting to regain this land,
and what constitutes professional and personal responsibility towards a dishonoured treaty? Land development
under colonial capitalism is based on stolen land and
labour stolen through slavery; it severed, and continues to
sever, people's connection with that land. But landscape
architecture often sees its disciplinary role as connecting
people with land, so how should it reckon with this
contradiction?

96 Jane Mah Hutton
→ Toronto, ON, Canada

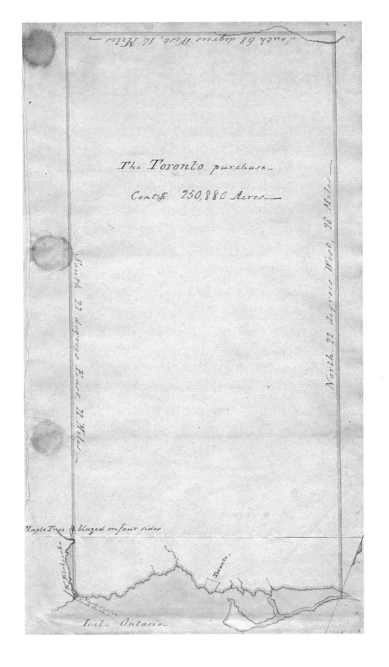

Map of the Toronto Purchase, 1805
Presented to the York Pioneers by William L. Baby in 1872, transferred to the Toronto Public Library in 1902. Part of the manuscript volume *Indian Treaties*.

Plant Names in Different Languages

Knowing the names, habits and cultural significance of many plants is an important part of landscape architecture. But what is any given plant – let's say your favourite species – called in languages that aren't English or Latin? What does this plant's name sound like in languages indigenous to this place? What does it sound like in your first language (if not English) or the different languages of people who live nearby? Do these names give new meanings to what you understand about this plant, to how you get acquainted with it? Do you or your ancestors have a relationship with this plant from different places you or they have lived? Did they bring it with them as they migrated? Considering these questions reminds us of the deep interdependencies that people have with plants for survival, culture and love. And also, imagine this plant without a name, outside of human conception.

97

Jane Mah Hutton
→ Toronto, ON, Canada

City of Toronto Archives, Fonds 124 f0124_fl0007_id0009

Kensington Market, Toronto, ON, Canada

Material Lives and Afterlives

As you specify materials in order to assemble a new landscape – whether soil mixes, stone, wood, steel or nursery
plants – consider also where they have been before and
where they will go afterwards. Picture how each has been
part of other landscapes: how a certain wood product
was a specific tree, that it was part of a habitat, a forest, or
maybe an industrial plantation. Picture how a metal, for
example, has taken different forms, from land to ore to alloy
to sheet metal to fabricated site furniture. Picture the
inputs and outputs of these stages, all that was required
to make those materials but that remains invisible in the
final product: the mining overburden, the water, the efflu-
ents, the herbicides. Picture the many afterlives they might
have – in landfills, compost piles, salvage yards or clever-
ly repurposed in new landscapes. Consider material spec-
ification as an engagement with these distant activities
and reflect on which ones should be strengthened and
which ones should not.

98 Jane Mah Hutton
→ Toronto, ON, Canada

City of Toronto Archives, Series 65, File 655, Item 5

Toronto brick works, city dump, 1960s

Who Else You are Working With

A landscape architect might work closely with a client, a public agency, a contractor, a nursery and a materials distributor. However, there are many other people participating in any landscape project, for example those who mine construction minerals, who care for plants, who clean surfaces and who demolish the whole thing later. All of these people work in different conditions – some hazardous, some unionised, some stigmatised, some valorised. In this web, landscape architects are privileged in certain ways, but they can also recognise that they are part of an exploitative labour system rather than external to it. Thinking about this connection can be a basis for solidarity, for seeing one's relationship to others' struggles. How does design work affect others' work – those who maintain a landscape or clean a space, for example? What design efforts could support meaningful work for those who recycle materials and cultivate landscapes?

99

Jane Mah Hutton
→ Toronto, ON, Canada

Salt piles at Wellington Street, Street Cleaning
Department, Toronto, ON, Canada, c. 1955–1956

What Will be Here after Your Lifetime

A landscape project can take a long time to be realised, designed and built – maybe five, ten or twenty years. This is significant in a career and a life. But consider this place beyond your lifetime, in a generation or three, after any awareness of authorship has disappeared. It is impossible to know what will happen here, but imagine. Will it be inundated, waterlogged and dispersed into the ocean? Will it be overgrown, host to unexpected new life that could thrive because of planetary climate change? Will it be demolished in ten years, landfilled and replaced with the products of a newer trend? Will it be remade and renovated beyond recognition but persisting in unseen, interesting ways? There are so many things that landscape architecture can't control; but at the same time, consider how you're putting into motion *something*. How does that *something* participate in long-term change in order to support life?

100 Jane Mah Hutton
→ Toronto, ON, Canada

Don River ice jam and flood, Toronto, ON, Canada,
28 February 1918

Solnedgangspladsen/ Sunset Space

The Sunset Space is a reflection that connects us to the sun and the universe, joined together with the present landscape of weather, wind and time, at dusk and dawn.

Gammel Skagen is a famous holiday village, known for its unique cultural environment developed around the original fishing community and the beautiful small houses that all turn protectively against the wind from the north-west. Here you will embrace a very special light. People have for many years been going to Sunset Space to enjoy the sight of the sun going down over the North Sea.

With this new transformation of Sunset Space the existing, incoherent space is gathered into a common square, comprising a large, 20-metre-diameter solar disc surrounded by several new sand dunes. Here, it is possible to experience the phenomena and ever-changing features of the landscape such as time, wind and weather at dawn and dusk.

The intention is not to let Sunset Space overshadow nature but instead to enhance it, by showing the movement of the sky, the wind and the sand. It thus becomes a space for reflection that connects us to the dynamics of the sun and the universe.

101 Kristine Jensen
→ Aarhus, Denmark

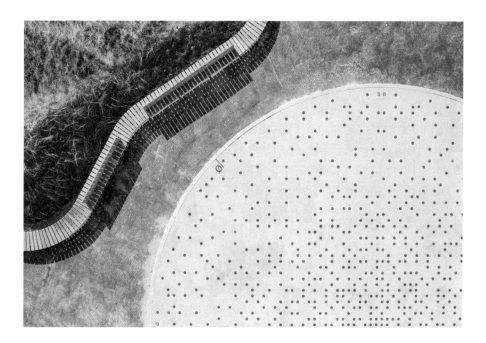

Solnedgangspladsen, Gammel Skagen,
Denmark, 2019
The solar disc is 20 metres in diameter and is adorned
with reflecting granite flakes, so that the clouds and the
rays of the sun glint off of it.

Around the large disc, a series of several small new
dunes are established as an extension of the coastal
protection off Gammel Skagen, which also provides shelter and the opportunity to linger. Landscape architects:
Kristine Jensen. Landscape & Architecture

Unesco World Heritage Site Jelling

Interweaving past and present to create a significant, memorable Viking place that continues to go with the ever-changing story of Jelling.

In the middle of the little town of Jelling, two grass-covered mounds rise majestically towards the sky, to a height of 8 metres and a diameter of 60 metres. Between the mounds are two giant rune stones and a white, chalk-washed medieval church.

The monuments tell of a time when Jelling became a significant area of royal power during one of the most essential periods in the history of Denmark: when Harald Bluetooth, the Viking, united the kingdoms of Denmark and Norway into one as a Christian nation.

Through simple landscape modelling, the masterplan interweaves the past and the present to form a significant and memorable place that communicates and processes historical layers and great new discoveries: a palisade fence with four sides, each one with a length of 360 metres, surrounding longhouses and a burial site formed as a longship dating from the year 980.

Based on an intention to identify and convey these new findings, along with the site's existing world-class heritage, the project breathes new life into the story of Jelling as a place of Viking-age supremacy and the cradle of Denmark.

102 Kristine Jensen
→ Aarhus, Denmark

UNESCO World Heritage *Site Jelling,* Denmark, 2014
The site forms a palimpsest: layer upon layer of different historical areas and importance.

Ground-laid concrete slabs form the base for hundreds of white concrete pillars that encircle the site, marking the approximate location of its original wooden stockade. The site is laid out as an open, green landscape filled with biodiversity from robust planting: a steppe – in geographical terms, an ecoregion characterised by grassland plains – filled with differently coloured thyme, grass and bulbs.

This field of grass and variation of thyme boasts a new identity along with a close connection to the town's existing plaza. Landscape architects: Kristine Jensen. Landscape & Architecture

Moesgaard Museum Landscape

Combining the old estate and the modern museum into a cultural-historical mosaic with the green roof has created a democratic green landscape for all times.

Moesgaard manor house (c. 1750) sits in a splendid landscape near the East Jutland coast, encompassing forestry, agriculture, hunting and fishing. The original buildings were erected on a 325-hectare property that today also houses a university, and the new additions sit amongst visible remnants dating back to ancient and medieval times.

With the new Moesgaard Museum building by architects Henning Larsen as well as the manor house, the 17,000-square-metre landscape was given a modern aspect that opened it up.

Today, the assembled cultural-historical mosaic of landscapes forms the new museum and contributes to a grand visitor experience. The museum's mediation does not restrict itself to the building's exhibits, separated from time and place, but is also present on site in the landscape itself.

Based on the inherent qualities of the place, new features add new ways to the old landscape: a historical and democratic landscape, which we can learn from, and which is important to safeguard in the future.

(103) Kristine Jensen
→ Aarhus, Denmark

Moesgaard Museum Landscape,
Aarhus, Denmark, 2015
Besides being a narrative museum landscape, Moesgaard is also an international exhibition venue as well
as a vibrant excursion spot and landscape of leisure
for the whole city of Aarhus. The open grassed space
of the roof has provided a whole new way of venturing
into the forest. Landscape architects: Kristine Jensen.
Landscape & Architecture

Marselisborg Park

Thinking of landscape as a whole: climate adaption combined with rehabilitation and recreation in a public park filled with new possibilities and biodiversity – all in a former park isolated and overused for car parking.

Around the Marselisborg Centre in Aarhus, a new recreational public city park has been established that combines health and rehabilitation with nature, biodiversity and climate adaptation.

For more than 100 years the Marselisborg Centre was an epidemic hospital with traditional, red-brick pavilion buildings and a classic, fenced-in garden. More recently the site's buildings were used as a rehabilitation centre, but the garden had been forgotten.

Marselisborg Park uniquely combines and meets the need for outdoor rehabilitation activities for the centre's users and for a comprehensive, recreational climate-adaptation effort for the local area. The project provides an example of how innovative rainwater solutions and biodiversity can become active participants in the design of recreational and social urban spaces. Nature's ever-evolving cycles are integrated into the park's operation and the appearance demonstrates a unique combination of rehabilitation and recreation in a public park filled with possibilities and biodiversity.

104 Kristine Jensen
→ Aarhus, Denmark

Marselisborg Park, Aarhus, Denmark, 2020
Green grassy rainwater beds and ditches store up the rainwater locally and lead it visibly through the park. Delay beds, with special vegetation and filter soil, purify road and roof water before it is passed on for evaporation and recycling.

By strengthening the park's richness of species, a greater level of biodiversity is created with several different habitat types. A flexible and robust urban nature is ensured, which is rich in resources and sensory experiences. Landscape architects: Kristine Jensen. Landscape & Architecture

J.C. Jacobsen's Garden

Making the layers of a private park accessible to the public by taking its botanical heritage to new heights amidst the post-industrial surroundings.

J.C. Jacobsen's Garden is an important part of the transformation of the former Carlsberg breweries into a sustainable green district in Copenhagen.

As part of this process, the brewer's old overgrown garden from 1847 is transformed into a public green lung related to the founder of Carlsberg Breweries, J.C. Jacobsen's own great passion for botany. Formerly it was a private, enclosed garden, that now serves as a beautiful public park that can be experienced along its meandering, historical paths as a green, recreational botanical space in the middle of the newly built-up city in between the transformed brewery.

The programming of this new space is based on a thorough process of registration and research into the different historical layers and functions of the site – and the transformation also reflects the history of its development across the various stages of the garden.

The garden has been brought into a new era of greater public use, in which climate adaption and accessibility are intertwined with the cultural heritage.

105 Kristine Jensen
→ Aarhus, Denmark

J. C. Jacobsen's Garden, Copenhagen, Denmark, 2018
In 1848, landscape gardener Rudolph Rothe created
one part of the romantic garden for the private use
of the founder of Carlsberg Breweries, J.C. Jacobsen,
where he could grow the trees and vegetation that he

brought home from his travels abroad. For 160 years,
this beautiful garden was closed to the public.
Landscape architects: Kristine Jensen. Landscape &
Architecture

Start with a Small Project and Execute it Yourself

Starting a design company as a young professional can be very challenging. You don't have enough experience and you don't have the necessary contacts to reach possible clients to gain that experience – a vicious circle.

It can also be frustrating to realise that despite your talents, in the design world nobody knows about you.

I believe a strategic way to start your career is through a self-managed, self-financed and self-executed project to back up your portfolio.

1. Find a few classmates, colleages or friends to participate in an experimental project.
2. Find a public space with sufficient footfall and/or exposure.
3. The design is very important: it should be controversial but smart, different, eye-catching.
4. Obtain the necessary permissions from the municipality/institution owning the space.
5. Make it happen using basic materials, techniques or any accessible means.
6. Record everything through photography/video – the final outcome *and* the "making of" process.
7. Show your work in as many online journals as possible.

This entire process should take no more than two months. Afterwards, you will have a decent amount of experience and a built project in your portfolio. In architecture and design, bigger is not better than built.

106 Marcial Jesus (100architects)
→ Shanghai, China

"Huellas Artes", Santiago, Chile, May 2014
This project was an ephemeral installation done by a group of fresh graduates in 2014. The project was self-managed and, self-financed, and stayed in place for *less than a week*.

Huellas Artes is an urban intervention that – just by intervening in the surfaces of the space, and demarcating areas and signals, suggesting functions and actions – transformed the existing space by adding stimulation and public functions. Designer: 100architects

The Age of Radical Differentiation and Surprise

The number of talented designers with so much more experience than you will be overwhelming. It is absurd to attempt doing "better" design with the same typologies that we have seen over generations. Maybe only a genius could.

To earn your place in the design world you need to differentiate yourself from what is being done now. This means that if you want to make a splash, whatever you offer as a designer needs to be unique in many more ways than having a functional purpose, meaningful narrative, economic design and good quality; what we are taught in university is not enough. You need to be radically different and surprising. You need to be pop and controversial, and incorporate experimental factors into your projects. Paradoxically, in the pursuit of this goal, you might touch the borders of the absurd. But that is OK. Often progress is built upon the unreasonable.

However, this doesn't mean doing weird design for the sake of being different. It means finding a niche, an aesthetic and a contrasting position that will make you surprisingly different from your competitors.

The reasonable man adapts himself to the world; the unreasonable one persists in trying to adapt the world to himself. Therefore all progress depends on the unreasonable man.[1] George Bernard Shaw

(107) Marcial Jesus (100architects)
→ Shanghai, China

"High Loop", Shanghai, China, 2020
High Loop is a project touching the borders of the absurd. The circulation routes are at the limits of the unreasonable. To design this project, we deliberately discarded the strategies that landscape architecture has traditionally used for this typology of projects. We risked being absurd in order to be radically different in our proposal. Designer: 100architects

1   Shaw, George Bernard (1903). *Man and Superman*, "Maxims for Revolutionists".

Play is Not Only for Children: The City of the Future Will Have Playgrounds for Adults

So far, our civilisation has understood our cities in a rather serious-minded and solemn way. Of course, everything has to be functional to the highest degree, but not everything needs to be so serious.

The concept *of the playground* is changing: it is not an enclosed space just for kids; instead, it has merged with the rest of the cityscape. Play is not only for kids; we all want to play in the city. The city is our *playground*.

You, as a landscape architect, should focus on more than just the ground. Interventions in the urban topography can happen in deeper and more experimental ways than hitherto, in order to create stimulating hardscapes that incorporate architectural shapes and programmatic functions, which should stimulate users by inviting them to interact with the space and objects directly and closely. Users of all ages should form an intimate link with the space and feel encouraged to slide, climb, lie down, play, hang out, take a selfie, rest, exercise etc.

(108) Marcial Jesus (100architects)
→ Shanghai, China

"Pixeland", Mianyang, Sichuan Province, China, 2018
Pixeland is a public-space project comprising a combination of different outdoor facilities in a single space – such as landscape features for resting and leisure, and playing features for kids and adults alike. Every "pixel" is a component with a different function on it. Thus, the functional pixels are arranged and combined in order to generate a stimulating hardscape of leisure activities. Designer: 100architects

Play Along with the Rules of the Culture of Overstimulation

How to call attention to and make your projects remarkable in this culture of disposability? It is too late to go "anti-system" – the world turns too fast and the trajectory is already traced. Instead, you can get ahead of the game by playing and knowing the rules.

Your "audience" today is an audience of experience seekers – people who prefer to invest in meaningful and memorable life experiences rather than anything else. Kids nowadays are not the same as those of past generations; they are exposed to, and used to, different kinds of sensory stimulations – even overstimulation. And finally, young adults also want to play in the city. In that regard, urban public spaces should now incorporate a form of recreation that meets the new needs of the current generation – their demands for increased stimulation and fantasy in experiences.

Your design for the cityscape will have to incorporate interactivity on many different levels: digital and technological interactivity on the one hand, physical and cognitive activity on the other. Always keep in mind the fact that humans learn by playing.

(109) Marcial Jesus (100architects)
→ Shanghai, China

"Creek play", Dubai Creek Harbour, Dubai, UAE, 2018
Conceived as a playful village, the proposal manifests as a 400-metre-long eye-catching playscape for the enjoyment of kids and adults alike. All the capsules are inspired by Dubai's arabesque shapes – such as those used in traditional doors, windows and other elements of vernacular-architecture – providing an immersive experience for the user. Each node comprises a conglomeration of capsules forming a stimulated village of fun, in which each capsule offers a different instant function such as sitting, swinging, sliding, climbing, lying down, playing and hanging out – all of them encouraging social interactions. Designer: 100architects

You Don't Come Up With Good Ideas, You Build Them

All too often, I have seen people of all ages waiting for *that* "good idea" to strike in their minds, believing that it will magically change their professional reality and signify the moment to "start" a business or launch a product etc. This is a rather unhealthy and damaging myth that has already lingered for long enough.

The truth is that professional success doesn't work that way. This is a principle that you should embrace for any future endeavour, from building a company to finding a concept for your project or product.

The fact is that almost 99% of successful companies, projects – or, basically, anything that is *good* – were really bad ideas at the beginning. However, they improved over time and gained complexity through a process of trial and error, incorporating new variables.

If you want to start a company, do it NOW. If you want to publish your work, do it NOW. If you want to launch a product, do it NOW. Maybe your output won't be excellent at the beginning – but the sooner you act, the faster you can start improving.

110

Marcial Jesus (100architects)
→ Shanghai, China

"Pegasus Trail", Chongqing, China, 2020

Before realising this project we designed and built many "ribbon-like" schemes. They were temporary installations all using the same strategy: a ribbon that bent and twisted to provide simple functions like seating and sliding. This strategy improved over time and gained complexity. The experience lay the groundwork for

Pegasus Trail, a 3,000-square-metre permanent public space following the same strategy but incorporating many complex functions – even including a "play circuit" for different age groups on the ribbon itself. This design would not have been possible without our earlier ribbon prototypes. Designer: 100architects

Knowledge

Trees have been associated with knowledge since ancient times. They are a part of the cosmos just as we are, although progress has led us to neglect the fact that we live in a shared space with Mother Nature. In a time of climate emergency, social conflicts and global pandemic the role of nature becomes apparent again. "We need to stop the war on nature," as US social theorist Jeremy Rifkin daringly stated years ago.[1] Our planet is revolting against our indifference, but nothing should be indifferent to us on Earth; as Pope Francis wrote in his encyclical *Laudato Si'*: "it's time we make peace with nature".[2]

We landscape architects are aware that knowledge is necessary to plant trees; we must understand the characteristics of a place in order to choose the seeds that can thrive there. A landscape project often has "deep roots", which helps us understand the multiple layers that shaped a particular environment and society; on the other hand it looks to the future with a holistic approach, not only as a superficial dressing of landscape but reflecting its body and feeding its soul.

111

Andreas Kipar (LAND)
→ Düsseldorf, Germany

Parco Nord, Milan, Italy
Parco Nord Milano is one of the most important European experiences of green belt in the metropolitan area. Parco Nord, the first "Italian step" by Andreas Kipar in 1985, is a continuous system of woods, meadows and rows of vines, enriched by ponds and watercourses.

1   Rifkin, Jeremy (2017). *A History of the Future – The World in 2025*. Lecture on 31 January 2017. European Central Bank (ECB).

2   http://www.vatican.va/content/francesco/en/ encyclicals/documents/papa-francesco_20150524_ enciclica-laudato-si.html.

Awareness

Our new horizon is the urban landscape, a territory of interrelations between nature, architecture and people where our responses and challenges will shape society. We can rethink our cities through regenerative transformation processes in which the environment plays an active role in reaching global sustainability goals. Back in the 1970s, Danish architect Jan Gehl put people on the main stage of urban life, fully aware that we are the environment and that it is only through us citizens that an intervention on open space can begin.

Even after decades ruled by the predominance of architecture, we still struggle nowadays to make our cities more liveable. "Landscape architecture teaches architects that living structures cannot be paralysed in static schemes," as Italian architect Bruno Zevi reminded us.[1] We must embrace visions that are able to manage conflicts and anxieties in our society by adopting more fluid urban patterns than hitherto.

112

Andreas Kipar (LAND)
→ Düsseldorf, Germany

Slogans. We live in a time of great challenges: amid climate emergency and the recent pandemic, we are all beginning to understand the need to "reset" and "reconnect" with nature. The urgency of this transformation is made even more pressing by the new "Greta generation", named after teenage Swedish activist Greta Thunberg, which is calling for action and asking for a strong repositioning of nature within our society.

1   Zevi, Bruno (1997). *Paesaggistica e grado zero della scrittura architettonica: consultazione internazionale e convegno*. Il Manifesto di Modena.

Perseverance

If it's true, according to author Jorn De Précy, that the garden created the man, then we need to constantly take care of our garden, cultivating its ecosystems and public spaces: we landscape architects plan development processes, we start interventions to heal damaged ecosystems and reconnect people with nature, we deal with the governance of our urban and rural areas. Perception is an essential component in starting long-lasting changes: in the 1980s, former West German Chancellor Willy Brandt imagined that the skies of the industrial Ruhr area would turn blue again. After more than 30 years of cultivation, we relish the completed regeneration of that German region's Emscher River and its cities. In 2010 "Essen for the Ruhr" was designated European Capital of Culture, and in 2017 the region's second-largest city was named European Green Capital. These events irreversibly shifted the mindset of people and paved the way for a new societal and political course. Green infrastructures are the future of our continent.

(113) Andreas Kipar (LAND)
→ Düsseldorf, Germany

Krupp Park, Essen, Germany

The Krupp Park project is a major redevelopment of the former Krupp steel factories located in Essen. The park's topography has been created using the debris of former industrial structures and soil excavated for the new buildings. Many trees were planted; rainwater from the newly constructed ThyssenKrupp headquar- ters building collected in a new pond; and naturalistic playgrounds were placed as social, green infrastructure for all citizens. The green infrastructure for the entire regeneration process in the Ruhr region led to Essen's successful nomination as European Green Capital in 2017.

Cultivation

We have been woken up from a long, careless sleep by a young Swedish girl who dared to remind us of our place on this planet. Her message reached citizens, activists, politicians and international organisations: "Natural resources aren't endless". So we need to start caring for our habitat, recalling what US philosopher Lewis Mumford declared over a century ago when initiating the City Beautiful movement.

The mission of landscape architects is the cultivation of productive landscapes that recover soil, water and biodiversity in a multidimensional way. Ecosystem services are key elements in improving urban wellbeing and providing a forward-looking, sustainable future. The new European Green Deal sets a milestone in our era: we need nature in order to build more resilient and prosperous communities.

(114) Andreas Kipar (LAND)
→ Düsseldorf, Germany

Krefeld Park, Krefeld, Germany
A cultivation process in Krefeld, Germany, based on a competition-winning proposal by international landscape-architecture studio LAND, is anticipated to last several years. Of the total site of 120 hectares, only 40 have been actually transformed; the remaining portion was kept as agricultural land. The park became the "frame" between the city's built-up area and the agricultural landscape, capable of giving space for new functions and of drawing a border, not through the houses but through the green of a row of pyramidalis oaks.

Prosperity

It's too late to be moderate! We need to act now to ensure a liveable environment for future generations. We can turn the greatest challenges of our time into opportunities: nature-based solutions are an effective tool for addressing environmental, social and economic issues; digitalisation and technological research can give a boost to shift us to a climate-neutral society. Our ambition is great: we deserve a better quality of life and we aspire to a fairer economy. Green infrastructure is the answer; it is a social matter because it concerns everybody, so we need to communicate this message clearly through co-creation processes and territorial cooperation. Landscape architects are mediators in this moment of global transition.

(115) Andreas Kipar (LAND)
→ Düsseldorf, Germany

A LIVING ORGANISM

Landscape Digitalisation is a global and cross-cutting phenomenon that has completely transformed our way of working and living. Public space has evolved according to this trend; digital technology allows us to expand, connect and monitor the landscape, but also reveals new opportunities for socialising, gathering and exploring. Digital landscape is a new dimension of the public sphere that deploys data-driven processes to tell new stories and share information about our environment.

Distinguish between Landscape Architecture and Architecture in Relation to Space and Time

Common to both disciplines is an anticipation of space and function – one might even say that it is necessary in order to envisage them.

It is the consideration of time that distinguishes landscape architecture from our neighbouring discipline, architecture. When an architect presents his or her newly finished building, it is at the high point of its life. For landscape architects the ultimate goal is still a long way off. It takes almost another two decades before their envisaged spaces become places and saplings have grown into trees.

Outside experts are often consulted for the planting design. However, I think that plant knowledge is essential for landscape architects themselves – not necessarily that of botanists but an awareness of the characteristics of plants with regard to the definition of space, structure and expanse; the expressiveness of a design repertoire that ranges from materiality and colour to the recurring rhythm of time.

116 Peter Latz
→ Kranzberg, Germany

It took 20 years for the tree canopy to close over at Landscape Park Duisburg Nord. A term you may recognise clarifies this: "establishment maintenance". Have you ever heard of anything like it for a building?

Management and maintenance in the park are based on experience. Two decades on the actors are changing; experience must be replaced by knowledge, the development of ideas geared towards the preservation of structure.

The park has "grown up", in a way that existed only in our heads and in drawings during the design process.

Explore the Information Content of the Landscape, and Distinguish between Introvert and Extrovert Spaces

Landscape consists of information: notations of actual, existing images and the connotation that exists only in the observer's mind. Following this theory, landscape design aims not only to implement elements of a high quality but also to provoke positive connotations.

The understanding that landscape and open space are composed of assembled bundles of specific information leads to an approach that distinguishes between introvert and extrovert spaces.

In introvert spaces the essential information must be derived from within the confines of the spaces themselves. This could comprise neutral stimuli or their intended manipulation. Some things are mere coincidence and reach beyond visual communication: the leaves of a tree rustle in the wind, water in the stream may sound like a melody and the twittering birds provide the background music.

Extrovert spaces are the exact opposite. They open up panoramas and draw attention to special features in the surroundings.

117

Peter Latz
→ Kranzberg, Germany

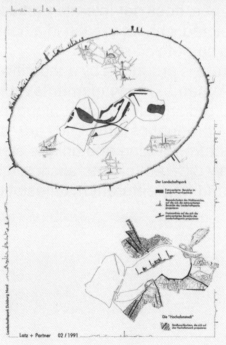

The experience of a space is not primarily shaped by the quality of the place but by its external information. Generally, the required images are selected and intrusive vistas, such as views of industry, are screened by landscape interventions. But it is precisely this industry that is considered to be constitutive of Duisburg Nord. That is why the park establishes a relationship with the panorama. Images on the outside are drawn into the park via the charging platform of Blast Furnace 5.

Distinguish between Structure and Form

Each project needs a structure that either exists or has to be generated.

The principle of structures cannot be changed or photographed but only extended or reduced, renewed or left to fall derelict. Structures can absorb spontaneous interventions without changing the essence of a scheme. They can even be a welcome divergence.

The opposite is true for the designed form. It appears as finished shapes, does not tolerate partition, can be fathomed and depicted, can be viewed in a holistic way, and relies on being something special.

The structure is produced by a repetitive configuration of the same elements. These elements represent the "normal" or the ordinary. However, unique, one-of-a-kind objects are the product of form. They are "special".

Both structure-forming and unique elements can have completely different characteristics, different material properties and thus different manifestations.

(118) Peter Latz
→ Kranzberg, Germany

What you need to consider: A concept that amasses only unique elements, aiming to repeat their special- ness, must inevitably fail – even if it is the express wish of the client. The goal should be the normal; it provides an essential basic structure in which special elements can be placed – as a symbol of culture, of nature or of social events.

In the Landscape Park Duisburg Nord, the crane bridge and the bunkers represent the serial while the gardens represent the exceptional.

Acquire a Feel for the Materials by Designing and Implementing at a Scale of 1:1

There used to be internships in Europe that offered the experience of working on a building site or in a tree nursery rather than in a landscape practice.

In order to make their significance tangible for the profession, I conducted one-week workshops for several years – held, among other places, in Saarbrücken during the construction of the city's Hafeninselpark.

The park's structure is abstract, practically invisible. It is based on the national grid of 20 by 20 metres. The work at a scale of 1:1 went even further in an area of the park where we incorporated recycling as part of the learning process. The construction material was reclaimed from building rubble that had been used to fill in the historic port. Students and apprentices were asked to formulate instructions for a 20-by-20-metre plot in a single sentence. Drawings and models were not permitted. They could, however, propose a mathematical formula, such as: "I subdivide the plot into ordered areas according to the Fibonacci sequence." They could alternatively be plant typologies, patterns of arrangement, sequences of operations, elements, planting principles or simply materials.

(119) Peter Latz
→ Kranzberg, Germany

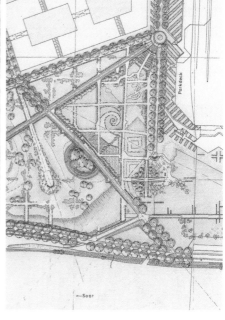

When we started digging into the wartime rubble in Saarbrücken's former river port some 30 years ago, we had no idea what it could be used for. Material was excavated and shaped into new elements. The "discovered" materials were spontaneously developed into something valuable and new: retaining walls, paths, steps and gardens. It was the adaptation of this once-destroyed material that generated creativity closely related to its physical form.

Be Conscious of the History of a Place and the History of Garden Art

Each place has its history. And so it seems obvious to understand design as the "invention" of information layers that overlap existing ones before form or expression are even considered. This means designing with the accepted and the disruptive, the harmonious and the inconsistent: a metamorphosis of the landscape without destroying the existing.

The history of our profession dates back to the gardens of Mesopotamia. In relevant courses of study, the history of garden art is part of the core academic curriculum. They favour examples that celebrate the representation of power and wealth.

Thus, it seems sensible to remind ourselves that most gardens are not designed by landscape architects. Lay movements play a major role in garden culture, formulating concepts of society in private gardens. They love to experiment, have a group-specific regard for new topics (self-sufficiency, health) and secure a broad sales market.

120 Peter Latz
→ Kranzberg, Germany

Landscape architecture must overcome the constraints of "form follows function" and make its mark with the power of images – images that endure.

The garden at Castello Ruspoli in Vignanello is from the early Renaissance period. Its vocabulary and form correspond to the aesthetic patterns of that time. The garden itself was limited to simple elements, but a new feature was that it opened out onto the landscape. The knowledge of the patterns of arrangement and technical know-how was passed down and applied over many centuries.

This place was the inspiration for me to design a garden along similar lines.

How to Listen

Sound is the essence and expression of life: birds singing in the trees, children singing in the streets, the ocean burbling in the harbour, trees whooshing in the backyard, cars howling along the highway.

The act of listening, and respect for the living, are always the starting point of my practice.

The place tells stories. I listen, understand and translate them into space. People talk and exchange news. I hear them, and implement their needs and wishes into my thoughts and design.

As landscape architects we need to know how to listen in order to shape cities for life. Cities that make people feel alive and allow them to connect to the world and other people around them. Cities that offer plants and animals a habitat. Cities that sound and vibrate.

121 Karoline Liedtke, Head of Landscape (Cobe)
→ Copenhagen, Denmark

Two women chatting in the garden in front of the Nordvest Library in Copenhagen. This northwestern area of Copenhagen is located between the lively and diverse urban district of Nørrebro and the suburban neighbourhoods at the edge of the city. The Library bridges the two and creates a meeting place. In an area dominated by very small apartments, the Library and its garden become an extension of people's homes, where residents line up for the daily 10 o'clock opening.

Latin

The Latin-based binomial nomenclature is a formal system of naming species of living things by giving each a distinct designation. Every plant has its very own name, and knowing these is our armamentarium for planning and the basis of our communication. Through it we can correspond beyond language barriers and make sure we mean the same thing. In a wider, interdisciplinary working environment it sometimes becomes a secret language that only an inner circle understands. I always enjoy the question marks on my non-landscape colleagues' faces when excitingly chatting with other landscape architects about different tree species and their special features.

Latin also means education, formality, tradition – and it is associated with the roots of Western culture. As landscape architects we are academically educated, and we should always make sure we study further throughout our careers. Extending our vocabulary is essential to generate innovation without brushing aside traditions.

122) Karoline Liedtke, Head of Landscape (Cobe)
→ Copenhagen, Denmark

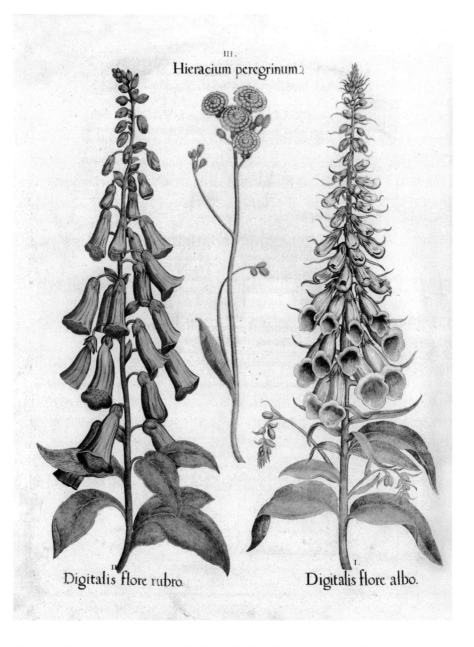

III.
Hieracium peregrinum

Digitalis flore rubro.

Digitalis flore albo.

Hortus Eystettensis is a codex produced by Nuremberg apothecary Basilius Besler in 1613 of the garden of the Bishop of Eichstätt in Bavaria, which changed botanical art overnight. The plates of garden flowers, herbs and vegetables, and exotic plants were depicted near life size, producing rich detail. Descriptions of the plants were in Latin and, remarkably, anticipated the binomial system by over 100 years.

Finding the Extraordinary in the Everyday

Copenhagen's bicycle culture has caught on as an icon of an attractive urban lifestyle that combines efficient, green mobility, healthy living, and leisure. And the common and daily use of the bike has raised a new set of challenges here: How to accommodate the 650,000 bicycles that exist in the city, without compromising the quality of urban space? How to shape public environments where infrastructure and public spaces are intertwined like urban organisms – where the ordinary structural needs to become extraordinarily beautiful?

The new university square in Copenhagen is arranged as a superimposed surface of hills and valleys, with room for 2,100 bikes underneath and space for social interaction on top. Circular holes bring light in these sacred-looking "bike-domes". Stairs, like vertebrae on a bowed spine, emerge on the outside surface, shaping stands for watching and listening. The university square becomes Copenhagen's biggest bike-parking lot and outdoor lecture hall.

(123) Karoline Liedtke, Head of Landscape (Cobe)
→ Copenhagen, Denmark

Karen Blixens Plads at the University of Copenhagen is one of the city's largest urban spaces. A hybrid of park and square, it is organised as a superimposed surface of human-made hills and valleys with room for over 2,000 parked bicycles inside the "hills". The plaza works as a campus landscape with an important functional role as well as being a recreational resource. The necessary infrastructure is turned into a three-dimensional student hang-out.

Copenhagen

In the 1990s, Copenhagen invested billions cleaning up its former industrial inner-city harbour, making it accessible to and swimmable for everyone. Some people have even begun to cultivate mussels and oysters in its waters – and the media have recently taken to reporting sightings of seals. Copenhagen has transformed itself from an industrial city to a city for life.

Smelling the ocean, having a notion of that natural water body and its creatures just beside where you live and work always awakens a certain yearning and thrill of anticipation in me. Just imagine the satisfaction, then, when jumping in and cooling down after a warm day. Or the melancholic mood when hearing a seagull. A sense of nature even in the densest city is magical. Conceiving of and introducing nature as a fundamental part of the city is an essential part of my understanding as a landscape architect. It puts us in context. We are only human after all.

124 Karoline Liedtke, Head of Landscape (Cobe)
→ Copenhagen, Denmark

The new Nordhavn is conceived as an urban archipelago or a series of dense neighbourhoods on the water. Along with green strips, new canals will be dug to enhance access and proximity to the water. The planning of "blue and green" city qualities precedes the planning of buildings. Strips of green spaces run from east to west. Movement through these sections is experienced as a diverse and varied journey. The public spaces vary from "urban green" in the south to "natural green" in the north.

From Where the Wind Blows

Denmark is a windy country. Wind here stands for leisure and sport. Having a boat and being out sailing is common, and forms part of most people's everyday lives and holidays.

Wind here means energy. Denmark can source almost half (47%) of its electricity consumption from wind power, and aims to reduce greenhouse-gas emissions by 70% by 2030.

Wind here creates a great awareness of moments and places when it finally stops blowing – places of the kind that are very much appreciated in most cities by the sea. Being conscious of where the wind blows from is essential when designing public and private spaces here.

And wind here is a cause for constant change. Denmark's coastlines are steadily eroding and reforming. Extreme weather events and rising sea levels are intensifying their forces, allowing these natural phenomena to become a threat to many communities and their property. And coastal-protection measures often seem to push the problem on to another place and time.

Here, some proper wind gusts might help us to clear our minds and to think anew. We need to find strategies *with* the wind and the waves rather than against them, letting natural dynamics become part of our cities and systems.

125

Karoline Liedtke, Head of Landscape (Cobe)
→ Copenhagen, Denmark

Copenhagen, a city based on reclamation and fortifications, seen from above. The transformation of Nordhavn (North Harbour) – the largest metropolitan development in northern Europe – continues Copenhagen's historic strategy of a step-by-step expansion into the surrounding sea. A way of solving problems (shortage of housing or/and creating new problems (disturbance and destruction of ecosystems)?

Make Landscape Multifunctional

Rural landscapes are often multifunctional, responding to human needs by adapting to climatic constraints and the limitations of natural resources. Citrus orchards in Iraq are planted under the high canopies of date palms to shelter them and optimise irrigation needs. Olive trees in the Mediterranean are inter-cropped with grain, doubling the economic benefits.[1] Multifunctionality takes on a new meaning in these regions today. Because the urgent need for economic and social betterment supersedes concern for environmental health, combining nature conservation with livelihood generation, environmental mitigation with development, is a sure way to address concerns for human and environmental wellbeing.

126 Jala Makhzoumi
→ Beirut, Lebanon

The high canopy of the date palms, *Phoenix dactilifera*, provides a microclimate for oranges planted underneath. Palm canopies shade the citrus fruit from the scorching summer sun. In the winter, the low angle of the sun allows it to infiltrate and warm the space under the canopy, which functions as a greenhouse. One irrigation network serves both palms and citrus trees.

1   Makhzoumi, Jala (1997). "The changing role of rural landscapes: olive and carob multi-use tree plantations in the semiarid Mediterranean", in *Landscape and Urban Planning*, vol. 37, pp. 115–122; Makhzoumi, Jala (2012). "Olive multifunctional landscapes in Cyprus: sustainable planning of Mediterranean rural heritage", in Elisabeth Conrad and Louis Cassar (eds.). *Landscape Approaches for Ecosystem Management in Mediterranean Islands*. Malta: Progress Press Ltd, pp. 219–234.

Diffuse Boundaries

Like ecosystems, landscape boundaries can be difficult
to determine. Processes and natural cycles transform,
sustain and bind urban, suburban and industrial techno-
ecosystems/landscapes with agricultural, natural
and semi-natural bio-ecosystems/landscapes.[1] Expansive readings of space/place cultivate a dynamic understanding of landscapes as networks and processes –
everchanging, rather than passive scenery. Breaching
boundaries frees designers from the polarised thinking
of urban/rural, nature/culture binaries to think, rather,
of landscapes as continua and ecological continuities.
Only then can landscape architects restore ecologies,
heal cultural discontinuities and contribute to human
rights and social justice.[2]

127 Jala Makhzoumi
→ Beirut, Lebanon

Landscapes flow across space and evolve over time. A spatially and temporally expansive reading of landscape encourages designers to look beyond the confines of a site, city and national borders. Spatial contiguities and ecological hierarchies of the global landscape invite a holistic, dynamic and networked reading and writing of landscape.

1   Bakshi, Trilochan S. and Naveh, Zev (eds.) (1980). *Environmental Education: Principles, Methods and Applications*. New York and London: Plenum Press.

2   Egoz, Shelley, Makhzoumi, Jala and Pungetti, Gloria (eds.) (2011). *The Right to Landscape: Contesting Landscape and Human Rights*. London: Ashgate. Makhzoumi, Jala (2018). "Landscape architecture and the discourse on democracy in the Middle East", in Shelley Egoz, Karsten Jørgensen and Deni Ruggeri (eds.). *Defining Landscape Democracy: Perspectives on Spatial Justice*. Cheltenham, UK and Northampton, MA: Edward Elgar Publishing, pp. 29–38.

Celebrate Seasonal Watercourses

Seasonal changes dictate alternative design sensibilities, and so designers should be alert to the temporality of landscapes. Parched earth and golden grasses in the summer are as beautiful as the verdant landscapes they morph into with the first autumn rains. Dry watercourses, important geomorphological features in arid and semi-arid ecologies, are favoured by humans and nature, which compete for their climatic sheltering and favourable environment. They also embody the seasonal absence/abundance of water and, whether a *wadi* in the desert or a small mountain stream, they are repositories of ecological memory, acting as nature's footprints. Swelling up with the first rains, flooding orchards and streets in the spring before drying out in the summer, seasonal watercourses ensure ecological connectivity, enhance the character of a place and render new landscapes meaningful to local communities.[1]

(128) Jala Makhzoumi
→ Beirut, Lebanon

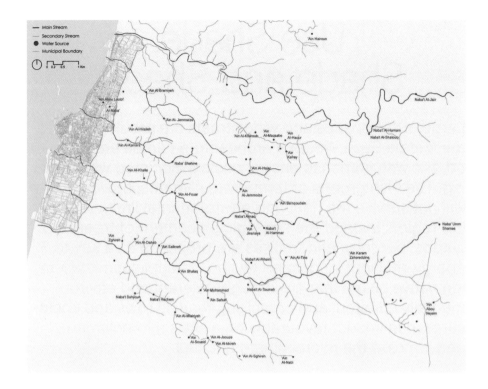

Coastal landscapes in Lebanon, such as that of Saida (Phoenician Sidon), are punctuated by rivers, streams and seasonal watercourses that extend beyond the municipal boundaries into the foothills. Local and national authorities discharge sewage into rivers and dry watercourses, the result of outdated engineering infrastructural solutions. The Saida Urban Sustainable Development Strategy (USUDS) recognises the ecological, spatial and socio-cultural role of seasonal watercourses, restores their ecologies and conceptualises them as linear parks – key components for sustainable urban greening.[2]

1   Makhzoumi, Jala and Al-Sabbagh, Salwa (2021). "A seascape planning approach: Reconceptualising coastal rivers and streams in Lebanon", in Gloria Pungetti (ed.). *Routledge Handbook of Seascapes*. Abingdon, UK: Routledge. In press.

2   Makhzoumi, Jala (2015). "The greening discourse: ecological landscape design and city regions in the Mashreq", in Robert Saliba (ed.). *Reconceptualizing Boundaries: Urban Design in the Arab World*. London: Ashgate, pp. 63–80.

Use Shade, Shade and Shade

Large urban spaces and wide streets are problematic in the Middle East. Western architecture *can* be emulated, but with immense energy costs associated with cooling. The lush greens of temperate climates, however, will not survive the heat and environmental limitations of the region. Instead the strategic placement of trees and shrubs, pergolas and trellises are proposed as a key to energy-efficient landscape design.[1] In application, selecting native plants that are drought-tolerant and environmentally adapted, and organising them in rows and enclosures, can impact favourably on a site's microclimate and improve the microclimate of cities.

129 Jala Makhzoumi
→ Beirut, Lebanon

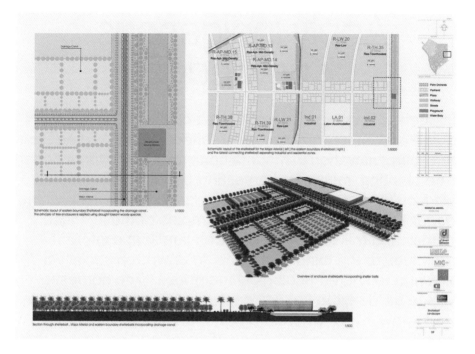

These modular tree enclosures are proposed by the landscape masterplan for a new city south of Basra, Iraq. The enclosures increase shaded ground area and shelter from dust-laden winds. *Ziziphus spina-christi* and *Prosopis spp*, both native to the region, are used because they are well adapted to the challenging site conditions and limited resources available for long-term landscape upkeep. The enclosed space doubles up as sheltered sport fields and/or locations for solar panels.[2]

1   Makhzoumi, Jala and Jaff, A. (1987). "Applications of trellises in retrofitting buildings in hot-arid climates". Proceedings of the International Building Energy Management Conference, Lausanne, Switzerland, pp. 460–466. Makhzoumi, Jala (1983). "Low energy alternatives for site planning through the use of trees in a hot arid climate", in S. Yannas and A. Bowen (eds.). *Passive and Low Energy Architecture*. Oxford: Pergamon Press, pp. 499–505.

2   Unit 44 (2014). Madinat al Nakheel. http://www.unit44.net/practice/ecological-planning/project-587353faf00518-62148024 (accessed 11.01.2021). *Landscape and Human Rights*. London: Ashgate. Makhzoumi, Jala (2018). "Landscape architecture and the discourse on democracy in the Middle East", in Shelley Egoz, Karsten Jørgensen and Deni Ruggeri (eds.). *Defining Landscape Democracy: Perspectives on Spatial Justice*. Cheltenham, UK and Northampton, MA: Edward Elgar Publishing, pp. 29–38.

Apply Indigenous Knowledge

Indigenous landscapes in villages and cities can inform, guide and inspire landscape architects in the Middle East. Terraced cultivation in mountainous terrain, multifunctional tree planting, rainwater-harvesting ponds in settlements, *wadi* cultivation, and vernacular irrigation systems such as *qanat* and *aflaj* are but some examples of these. Place names and folk language, rich with landscape inferences, are clues to the history of place, to unwritten social values and to shared ecological memories.[1] The domestic village garden, the *hakura*, captures the essence of inherited knowledge[2] wherein production and pleasure are combined to optimise the use of water, and enclosure and shade are prioritised to temper the climate.

(130) Jala Makhzoumi
→ Beirut, Lebanon

A vernacular domestic garden in Beirut (circa 1900) is inspired by the village *hakura*. The space of the garden is "full" and shaded – a place that engages the senses with an abundance of shapes, colours and scent. The *hakura* exemplifies the description of paradise in the Bible and the Quran as a shaded landscape with a diversity of fruit trees. Beirut's vernacular gardens are the antithesis of the Western, modern garden designs that came to replace them, which prioritised open space and form over productivity and climatic sheltering.

1 Makhzoumi, Jala (2009). "Unfolding landscape in a Lebanese village: Rural heritage in a globalizing World", *International Journal of Heritage Studies 15*(4) pp. 317–337.

2 Makhzoumi, Jala (2008). "Interrogating the hakura tradition: Lebanese garden as product and production", *International Association for the Study of Traditional Dwellings and Settlements*, Working Paper Series, vol. 200, pp. 50–60.

Taking in the Very Essence of the Territory

As landscape designers, when first visiting a site – while walking and experiencing the land that will be transformed and eventually improved with our work – we should breathe in its very nature: the inherent qualities of this land and the original physical arrangement of its natural elements. At this moment (the one we should know is the most revealing and inspiring) we need to be open to the beautiful and generous art of observation, intimately connected to the gift of listening to nature. Let the earth and the water talk – the trees and the silence, too. Once we take in all that is there and all that is not, we can put a finger on it; then, our hands can go to work, our thoughts and our drawings progress – not before. It is the specificity and the essence of a place that will provide us with a true muse for our proposal. Let's be awake.[1]

131 Teresa Moller
→ Santiago, Chile

Lo Curro, Santiago de Chile, Chile
As part of an old water-collection system fed by local
streams, the site had a series of abandoned pools and
tanks. They were restored and rebuilt with stone to receive the water at different levels, taking advantage
of the natural 15-metre change in elevation. In the
past, water timidly ran down the natural hill, getting
wasted; after clearing up the site it was rediscovered
and retained in the rebuilt tanks and ponds; now, as
it keeps falling and being caught, still hidden by trees
and shrubs, its constant soothing sound reveals that it
is and it always was there.

1   Translation by Jimena Martignoni.

Dumping All Preconceptions and Orthodoxies

As designers, we need to be free. We need to empty ourselves of all preconceived notions and ideas, trends and orthodoxies. Freedom, as we know, takes much courage. In the same way, we need to be courageous in order to get rid of everything we tried in former projects and everything other designers tried in theirs – not as an act of arrogance but as one of connection with the here and now. We need to ask ourselves, "Is this a valid idea for this place?" Sometimes a barely noticeable intervention is the only answer for a given place, a subtle landmark or an element that has a purpose and an intangible sense of life. In this way, we are able to create a pact between design and nature, the man-made and the pristine. Our work, then, becomes a unique creation in response to a unique place.[1]

132 Teresa Moller
→ Santiago, Chile

Parque Villarica, Villarrica Woods, Chile
In southern Chile, a circular pond made of stone receives the rainwater to feed an irrigation system and
creates reflections of the local woods and the light
coming through the foliage. Nothing else seems to be
required by the site.

1   Translation by Jimena Martignoni.

Incorporating the Needs and the Customs of Others

We are designers, yes, but that does not make us protagonists. We need to think about the people who will be using, enjoying, inhabiting and experiencing the designs we place on nature. What are the dreams, the tastes and the expectations of these people? What do they take pleasure in? And once we can identify this, we need to be able to relate to it. The truth is that our work is not for us but for them, not for the sake of design or for being published. Our appreciation for others – together with the capacity to incorporate our own "emotional baggage", creativity and knowledge – is the measurement that will indicate how good the result of our work will be. The more we appreciate their needs and expectations, and the more we connect our thoughts and proposals to them, the closer our project will come to being great.[1]

133 Teresa Moller
→ Santiago, Chile

Punta Pite, Zapallar, Chile
This is about a path that draws an itinerary through the cliffs and takes the visitor closer to the ocean, with no precise direction. Instead, the composition invites walkers to create their own way and to be surprised by the pieces that appear on the natural rocky surface. The path appears only at those spots where it is needed to help visitors keep walking and, in order to announce how to continue, isolated pieces are placed as signs in the landscape.

1   Translation by Jimena Martignoni.

Designing with the Less Intrusive Geometry

Our work as designers should be something that reads as a loving interaction and not as a careless intervention. For this, we have to ask ourselves how to approach a project and how we can touch the earth with our work. If we tried to picture our design as seen from the air, and then how people would walk the site without it losing its distinctive character, we would find that working with subtle elements and compositions was our most natural choice. Lines are the subtlest way for humans to touch the earth; they are a sign of the conversation between humankind and nature from the beginning of times (water-distribution channels, nomad routes, fences). They are the healthiest and least intrusive design element that we can use to relate to nature. However, even a line has to be there for a reason; you don't build a bridge if there is no river to cross.[1]

134

Teresa Moller
→ Santiago, Chile

Punta Pite, Zapallar, Chile
Underneath a beautiful canopy of existing cypress
trees and framed by the water-receiving stones designed by sculptor Gerardo Ariztía, a runnel made of
local stone appears as a subtle line in the landscape
and a place of encounter.   1   Translation by Jimena Martignoni.

Activating Economical Thinking and Processes

As designers of an era in which sustainability is the only answer for a struggling planet, we need to think and plan with an economical perspective. This is about being aware of (and grappling with) the fact that there aren't enough resources to satisfy all our needs and desires. We need to make friends (responsible friends) with the concept of scarcity–scarcity not only of natural resources such as water and land but also of those apparently less important, yet indispensable, ones such as time and funding. Today, the more we commit to economical thinking and design, the timelier our project will be. In turn, the less presumptuous our project, the stronger people's response will be to the places created because they will feel freer and will act more naturally in them–becoming, themselves, part of the scenery.[1]

135 Teresa Moller
→ Santiago, Chile

Venice Biennale 2016, Arsenale, Venice, Italy
Catch the landscape is an art installation made of discarded pieces of travertine found in some recently discovered quarries of northern Chile. The Biennale's curators decided to keep this composition at the site as a permanent exhibit. Travertine is a choice that seeks to honour Italian history and also to create an eternal conversation between the old and the new world. These pieces seek to silently call the visitor in a natural invitation to rest and to be there by the water, also understanding this element as a key component of Venice.

1   Translation by Jimena Martignoni.

Common

"Common" denotes a space shared between several relationships of beings in the world – whether mineral, vegetal, animal or human. Common is the regulating and fundamental principle of public space, in the sense that it is not specific to a particular type of population. A democratic society is consolidated and nourished by its ability to "do, be and dream" together. Limiting public spaces to comply with the social norms of the moment is part of the criteria of comfort and security of a society inclined towards total control. The Living shows an ingenuity that is out of all proportion to what our brains can grasp. When one party fails, another party mobilises to take over. Each party has the capacity for versatility in order to compensate for the fragility of the other. The potential of a place, of an installation, resists the single thought of a single interpretation for the benefit of the common good.

136 Catherine Mosbach
→ Paris, France

Spontaneous performing: "Louvre Lens" forecourt, 2016
The landscape project weaves links between populations and living places. It indicates the potential links between individuals and communities – a humanistic issue. It is an indicator of a common good whose creative dimension should not be subordinated to standard-isation. Spaces – outside of standards – nourish people's minds, and are as much markers of initiatives for tomorrow's populations. Landscape work has the power to bring us all together, wherever we are, to share amenities, imaginations, sensitivities – to welcome a better life for further generations through the ages.

Design

Designing a programme on a site initiates a dialogue between a community and other temporalities: animal, plant, soil, water, sound, air and light. A dialogue nourishes the dialectic between what is known, delimitable at the moment of the facts, and what is in continuous formation of a world where human beings are only one part of a larger system. A child draws before knowing how to read and write. Drawing unfolds the spectrum of the imagination, of the reception of the one who emits as well as of the one who receives. Imagination is the leaven of creation, of the encounter between one world and another, between an individual and a group. The world "delivers" to our beings only if we establish principles of deciphering. The landscape architect has the privilege of playing with the real being incarnated. Let's not lock it into pre-established patterns.

Catherine Mosbach
→ Paris, France

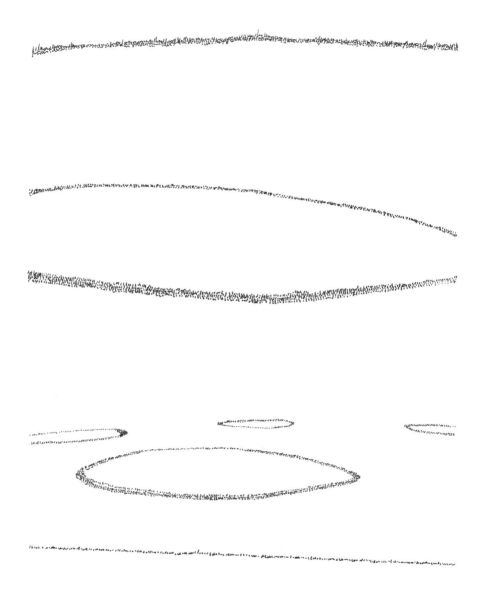

Lithosphere design, Central Park, Taiwan, 2017
The line folds and unfolds in a whirlwind until it "sets". Fluid dynamics are represented by a bundle of lines or vectors. Drawing intentions translates a thought, a way to play with the hazards without losing the heart of the subject. The design is a guide; it is revisited until the last moment with the taking of shape of the material. Design is essential, like the words assembled for a text. No project without drawing (purpose): milestones, measures, rhythms to approach what you want to achieve and unfold.

Imagination

Imagination is a vast field, still fallow in the limited universe of life sciences. It is only manifested through the perception of what comes to it from outside of an incarnated envelope. Yet its exteriors pass through the senses, which, according to Rudolf Steiner, would be approached by Speech – Taste – Sound – Balance – Meditation – Vision – Motion – Identity of the I – Touch – Freshness – Smell – Vitality. The works of landscape architects are intended for a public, drawn from all cultures. The orchestration proposed for a place must be able to accommodate and nourish all its layers; it is a question of the capacity of being on this Earth. Landscape architects have the duty to nourish the imagination of whole populations in order to cultivate their singular resources to live in this world.

138 Catherine Mosbach
→ Paris, France

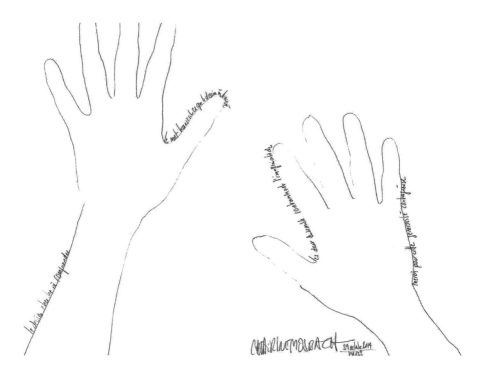

Tribute to Michel Corajoud, 2014

Imagination takes hold of the nebula of phenomena and transcribes it in the hope of cultivating some of the wonders of the world. It unfolds the possible. It is receptive to what is not yet delimited, regulated by the norms of the present time. The landscape project initiates the foundations of an always-open dialogue – exposed to the temporalities of the weather and the passing of time – offered to the appetite of the curious being that seizes it. A landscape project is accomplished from the moment it invites people to marvel at the world beyond technical performance.

Micro Macro

The world that welcomes us is multiscalar, incorporating the scale of our daily environment and that of the universe – constellations, galaxies – which exceeds our human temporalities. Initiating a "fertile" canvas for capturing the processes of the living implies becoming aware of the invisible at the origin of the visible. Technologies for capturing images and waves – visual and sonic – at all scales – micro and macro – have unfolded spectrums of knowledge. Becoming aware of the micro "biological" world is a prerequisite for any landscape architect. Questioning the singularities of a site at the scale of its "initial" earth–sea formation, above and below the surface, allows the "tailor-made" transcription of a programme for a place. A landscape project should be unique for one and only one place. The infinite reproduction from one part of the globe to another of dominant models, whatever the site invested in, is a colonial paradigm.

139 Catherine Mosbach
→ Paris, France

"In the net of desires", Milan Triennale, Italy, 2016
Landscape architects play with infinite scores. They bring them to the forefront of the "market of the real" on their space–time scale. Their universe of fabrication of the Living crosses the visible and invisible layers from the macro to the micro. They would be this su-
pra medium that, through morphogenesis, generates mineral, vegetal, animal formations from a skein of microorganisms. The possibility is offered to all and open to those who take the risk. Designers: Catherine Mosbach, Ovvo Studio

Transmission

"Passing on" means bequeathing to the next generation the virtues of living well together. It is accepted and easily apprehended that monuments are an integral part of such legacies, and the works of landscape architects are most often destined to have a limited duration. The transmission of a landscape project's spirit is defined as early as its conception and implementation. The work of a landscape architect is also defined by the management of continuously arising formations in a particular place. This dimension is random, depending on the actors involved in the process. Yet, it is essential if our present-day selves want to leave a sensitive impression for subsequent generations. It is admitted that nothing is ever certain, that everything is constantly being built. This capacity to build through drawing with the Living must be cultivated. Not to cultivate it is a denial of civilisation itself.

140 Catherine Mosbach
→ Paris, France

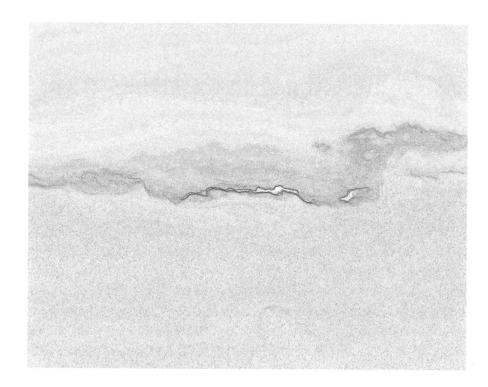

"Nebulosities", sky, Dublin, Ireland, 2017

The alliance of the elements on Gaia – water, air, earth – dictates the instruments of a mode of producing landscape, and exposes the assets highlighted in a singular place. Independently of the ingredients mobilised to respond to one function or another (capturing rainwater, limiting the resurgence of seeds, welcoming wildlife, and so on), these polarised masses indicate the interfaces and migrations among them. They designate operations of supportive environments – the movement and nature of one impacts on the movement and nature of the other – for lands hosting singular beings.

Landscape Architecture is a Practice of Care

The activity of caring, in the words of scholars Joan Tronto and Berenice Fisher, includes "everything we do to maintain, continue, and repair our 'world' so that we can live in it as well as possible. That world includes our bodies, our selves, and our environment, all of which we seek to interweave in a complex, life-sustaining web."[1] This woven web of life is on full display in public spaces and landscapes, where the interdependencies between species, environments, ecology and society demonstrate the fundamental interconnectedness of planetary inhabitation.[2] In the context of today's compounding environmental and social crises, it is increasingly urgent for landscape architects to cultivate an ethic of care in order to nurture robust, resilient and just spaces and ecologies. The practice of landscape architecture carries the agency and responsibility to bring about necessary changes – and to do so, we must learn to listen, take care and act.

141 Aisling M. O'Carroll
→ London, United Kingdom

"Parliament of Plants", Studio Céline Baumann, exhibited at "Twelve Cautionary Urban Tales", Matadero, Madrid, 13 February 2020–31 January 2021
In "Parliament of Plants", woody, leafy and flowering beings convene in an urban, parliamentary forum. Endowed with political agency, the plants shape an alternative democratic debate based upon mutual care and support. This vegetative administration takes decisions for the common good, informed by its knowledge of ecology, inclusion, tolerance and diversity.

1   Tronto, Joan C. and Fisher, Berenice (1990). "Toward a Feminist Theory of Caring", in Emily K. Abel and Margaret K. Nelson (eds.). *Circles of Care: Work and Identity in Women's Lives.* Albany, NY: State University of New York Press, p. 40.

2   Fitz, Angelika and Krasny, Elke (2019). "Introduction", in Angelika Fitz and Elke Krasny (eds.), *Critical Care: Architecture and Urbanism for a Broken Planet.* Cambridge, MA: MIT Press, pp. 12–13.

Take Time to Appreciate the Otherness of Plants

Plants are alive, dynamic and unpredictable. They are capable of forms of adaptation, reproduction, transformation and a longevity completely foreign to us as humans. Their structure, foliage, fruit, seasonality and aesthetics offer endless fascination and variety with which to work. Designing with a raw material imbued with its own intelligence, agency and vitality requires a nuanced mediation between designer, site and material. The resulting relationships may get their start in the development of a project on paper but they continue well beyond that point, and beyond a project's "completed" construction on site. As landscape architects we have to take the time to learn *from* plants as well as learn to work *with* them, to appreciate the "otherness" of their vibrant, vegetative vitality rather than seeing them purely through our own human perspective. We have to commit to the long-term relationship that working with plants entails.

(142) Aisling M. O'Carroll
→ London, United Kingdom

Forest profile from Saint-Élie, French Guiana, Francis Hallé, ink on tracing paper, 162.5 × 145 cm (undated) French botanist Francis Hallé has spent his life drawing trees in order to become familiar with and understand the interconnected complexity of rich forest communities and individual plants. The slowness of observing and drawing allows him the time to patiently discover a tree's form and structure. His forest profile captures not only the "architecture" of individual trees but also the vitality of the whole tropical rain forest system.

Learn to Read Multiple Histories

When designing with landscape, there is no such thing as a "blank slate". We are always working from an existing condition that holds memories, meanings and multiple histories. Urban-landscape historian Thaïsa Way describes landscapes as being "thick with history".[1] Our ability to design responsibly and well for the future requires engaging with the interwoven pasts that each site contains. Landscape architects have to be dexterous and resourceful in searching out these histories of place – particularly as they require us to see a site from perspectives other than our own. We have to develop appropriate tools and techniques for representing, comprehending and communicating the complex layers of a site's history in our design process. This task is far more challenging than working from a *tabula rasa*, but it leads to more powerful, meaningful and resilient spaces.

(143) Aisling M. O'Carroll
→ London, United Kingdom

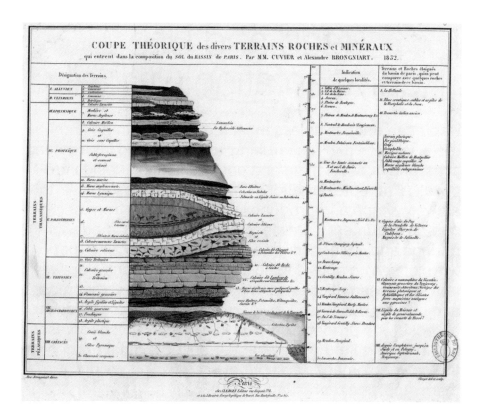

"Theoretical geological section through the
Paris Basin", Georges Cuvier and Alexandre
Brongniart, 1832
In their study of the Paris Basin, French geologists
Georges Cuvier and Alexandre Brongniart read the
landscape's history stratigraphically through its section,
wherein geological layers record chronological time.
A site's convoluted histories can be found in various
forms: in books and written accounts; embedded in its
geological, vegetative and built materials; or captured
in its representations and stories, and in the memories
of its inhabitants.

1   Way, Thaïsa (2020). "Why History for Designers?
(Part 1)", *Platform*, 2 March. https://www.platform-
space.net/home/why-history-for-designers-part-1
(accessed 02.04.2021).

Read and Use Representation Critically

Representation is an essential tool for landscape architects. We use it in researching, analysing and interpreting sites, and in developing and communicating design proposals. But representations are not simply descriptive, they actively shape and produce landscapes. Far from being neutral documents, drawings, sketches, maps, models, renderings and collages frame knowledge and construct ways of seeing and reading sites. To use Donna Haraway's term, representations are "meaning-machines" that record and convey the ideas, power relations and interactions of those who produced them.[1] In a field in which representation is ubiquitous, landscape architects must recognise the power of images and our own agency in producing them. Applying representation critically as a tool for design entails considering the role that instruments, materials, technology and our own intentional perspective play in producing representations; the ideas embedded within them; and, ultimately, the landscapes that they shape and generate.

(144) Aisling M. O'Carroll
→ London, United Kingdom

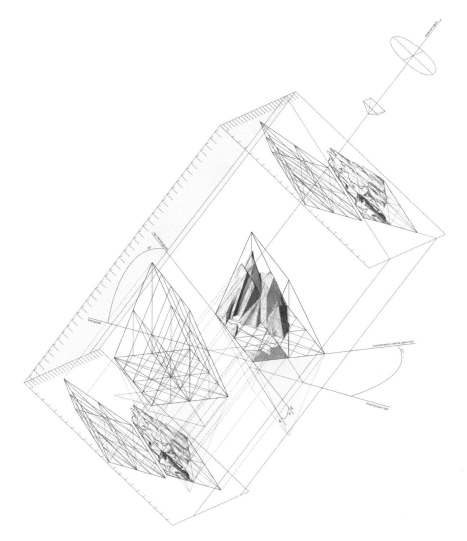

"Reconstructing the Dent du Requin",
Aisling O'Carroll, 2019
Using a combination of digital and analogue techniques, this drawing reconstructs a peak in the Mont Blanc massif from a 19th-century drawing by French architect, Eugène-Emmanuel Viollet-le-Duc. Although the architect's simplification of the peak to a crystalline form may seem harmless, the theory of a perfect natural order that underlies the drawing carried far-less-innocent claims of power and superiority that extended to nation, race and architecture. By reconstructing the errors and distortions of Viollet-le-Duc's sketch, the new drawing confronts both his idealised view of geology and its limitations.

1   Haraway, Donna J. (1984). "Teddy Bear Patriarchy Taxidermy in the Garden of Eden, New York City, 1908–1936", *Social Text* 11 (Winter 1984–1985), p. 52.

Embrace
Not Knowing and Enjoy
Finding Out

Landscapes are complex things. They perform social, ecological, infrastructural and political functions (to name just a few). In designing these spaces landscape architects have to navigate a field of varied interdisciplinary domains. Design thinking itself requires a wide breadth of diverse knowledge – and yet, despite being equipped with that knowledge, when responding to complex environmental, social and engineering problems we often don't have all the answers. Rather, one of the most important skills of a landscape architect is to identify which questions need to be asked and what other expert knowledge and input is needed. This means having conversations, crossing fields of expertise, testing and experimenting, working with other specialists, and recognising that the best designs are co-produced by multiple individuals. In order to deliver projects that are innovative and effective, we need to understand the language of different fields, and then lead through collaboration.

(145) Aisling M. O'Carroll
→ London, United Kingdom

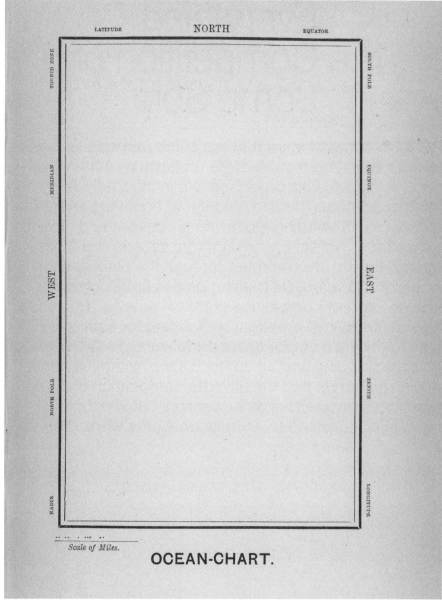

"Ocean-Chart" (The Bellman's Map), Lewis Carroll, 1874 In Lewis Carroll's *The Hunting of the Snark*, the crew praises the Bellman's map for being "a perfect and absolute blank!" The ocean-chart, free of the "merely conventional signs" of cartography, presents the sea as an open, ambiguous territory to cross. The design process can feel similarly uncharted – an interdisciplinary terrain to get productively lost in. As landscape architects we need to be comfortable enough to dive into unknown territory and lead a project to a satisfactory resolution.

Everything is a Competition of Some Sort

We have come to learn that the entire universe is dynamic, not static. One aspect of life on Earth as it has developed is that all living organisms are in competition for one thing or another. This is a function of acquiring energy and nutrients to fuel ongoing life processes and growth – for better or worse. *Everything* from viruses and algae, to mosses and invertebrates, through the plant and animal kingdoms to scientists battling viruses and each other is in one sort of competition or other – whether for sunlight and space, sexual propagation, funding for a project or time to think a bit more about one's work. It's OK, however. It keeps us going and on our toes. One nice thing about design and art is that the ultimate competition is not with one's peers, ancestors or successors but with oneself, one's own ideas and to improve on earlier work.

146 Laurie Olin
→ Philadelphia, PA, USA

Competitions. Competitions offer an opportunity to think and work conceptually. The invited competition for Berlin's Memorial to the Murdered Jews of Europe was won in 1997 by the concept design of Peter Eisenman and Richard Serra. Laurie Olin joined the team, and later Serra withdrew in 1998. The German Government decided to proceed in 1999, and fundraising began. Construction commenced in 2003 and the memorial opened to the public in 2005. This is one of 18 competitions Olin and Eisenman have collaborated on to date, a handful of which have been built.

Water Still Runs Downhill – Thank Goodness

While others (architects and clients) commonly try to make things flat, landscape architects know that water moves and that it is easy to improve life with good, positive drainage. Pumps and other mechanical devices will always need maintenance and frequently break down, but good old gravity is your friend and will do a lot of work for you if you do a good job of grading (setting the levels well). Plus, you can have a lot of fun playing with how water moves and the nature of the path it takes. Water is the lifeblood of the Earth. Designs that have water invariably please and attract humans and other animals. We love it and can't stay away. It is mercurial, rarely at rest. It can be serene, lively, playful, or intimidating and dangerous. People, young and old, almost always walk up to its edge if they can and stick their toe or hand in it. Treat water with respect. Be generous and think carefully about how you wish to accommodate interaction with it.

147) Laurie Olin
→ Philadelphia, PA, USA

Water. Many of our favourite places contain water in some form. It's hard to keep people out of it, especially children – so its situation and design are important. It moves, reflects and looks best in sunlight. We have done countless water features – and designed esplanades and overlooks just for the pleasure of being near and viewing it. Clients often find it worrisome and resist, but it's worth fighting to include it. Here, people cool off on a hot summer day at the National Gallery of Art Sculpture Garden in Washington, DC.

If You Can't Get Soil That is Adequate in Quality and Character, Forget about Planting Anything

It's all about the $100 hole and the $10 tree. Without proper drainage, the correct pH and the right sort of nutrients and microbial life, plants are guaranteed to struggle and die. The world is full of failed and struggling landscapes that ignored or didn't meet this basic need. What others call dirt, you know is *soil*. This also means you must do everything possible to prevent its erosion and loss, as well as to avert its contamination – often enough caused by the very contractors who are building your work. This is truly a case of quality – often over quantity, although it matters that there is enough soil and that it is fed (replenished) as plants draw on it and use its minerals and nutrients for their structure, growth and remarkable photo-chemical processes.

148 Laurie Olin
→ Philadelphia, PA, USA

Soil. Transplanted old olive trees, Cupertino, CA. The combination of soil, excavation and planting mix is critical, and is where a project can fail. The future success of this planting has everything to do with the soil – how well it drains, the balance of structure with texture, whether the roots can enter the surrounding land without becoming trapped in what amounts to a pot with hard sides.

No one – except the labourers and landscape architect – is particularly interested in this, but everyone sees the result – sometimes tragically, but when done well: gloriously.

"Native" Plants are on the Move

Many species on every continent have been coming or going like immigrants and emigrants throughout history. The world is dynamic, not static, and climate change is a fact, the biggest problem facing the entire population of all the creatures on the Earth – whether plant or animal, on land or in the sea. So-called "native plants" are on the move again, as in earlier eras (ice ages etc.). Pay attention. In the USA, climate zones have already been revised from what they were for the past hundred years – and most likely will need to keep being readjusted: don't "hang your hat" on soon-to-be-extinct plants in your region. Think instead about what is most likely to succeed in a decade or two, which is just the blink of a landscape's eye. Where will such future successful "residents" be from, and how do you get hold of them, now – not after it is too late? Beware of ideologies – even supposedly ecological ones – when facing natural processes, new facts and crises. Stay open-minded. Think globally and act locally.

149 | Laurie Olin
→ Philadelphia, PA, USA

New and old "natives". A mixture of Mediterranean, southwest-desert and Bay Area native plants. With the deepest drought in a century expected to continue and possibly worsen, many traditional and familiar regional plants are struggling and may not survive the decade. Experimenting with a selection from elsewhere to fill particular niches and purposes seems an appropriate response. Planting has always been an experiment: worldwide, plants, insects and animals on land and in the sea have been moving – and experimenting – for survival. All our natives – people and plants – arrived here from somewhere at different times.

Thanks to Entropy, There is No Such Thing as Maintenance-Free Anything

Just as we take care of our clothing, houses, cars and children or else they develop problems, fall apart or become unruly – so, too, it is with the environment. You should fire any client who demands a maintenance-free or foolishly low-maintenance design. A handsome well-built landscape will usually hold up better and receive more care than a cheap one. People usually take better care of a Mercedes or an Armani suit than they do a Volkswagen or blue jeans. So, too, with landscape. Short-term cost savings are anathema to landscape design.

150 Laurie Olin
→ Philadelphia, PA, USA

Everything requires maintenance, just as there still is "no free lunch" in society or ecology The desire for beauty with little or no investment in its care and maintenance is an affliction of contemporary Western society. It is one of the landscape architect's tasks to educate those we work with and for. Time is a deep and eventful aspect of our medium. With time things grow and blossom; with time also comes entropy: things age and fall apart. To avoid living in a ruin or wilderness, effort, time and investment must be made in care and maintenance. How much is enough depends upon the situation.

Bitches Get Stuff Done

It's time for women to lead the design fields forward. Time for landscape architects to shed our reputation as mediators and peacekeepers brought in to plant, buffer and beautify; time to cut through the traditional boundaries of private practice and the aestheticisation of the status quo. Our circumstances – racial injustice compounded by a pandemic; warming, expanding oceans; the "sixth extinction" of biodiversity – require more of us. The climate-feminist movement models a path forward, a more radical conception of landscape activism. Landscape architects have much to learn from social movements. Racial and climate justice are inextricable, and both help us define spatial goals that question entrenched notions of property and ownership and challenge the powers that control the built environment – engineers, planners, developers, elected officials and donors. As landscape architects in a climate-changed world, our role is to forge more transformative connections in the public realm at every scale. Not everyone will like you in this process. That's fine.
To quote comedians Tina Fey and Amy Poehler[1] and, more recently, US Congresswoman Alexandria Ocasio-Cortez: "Bitches get stuff done."[2]

151 Kate Orff (SCAPE)
→ New York, NY, USA

ALL WE CAN SAVE

Truth, Courage, and Solutions for the Climate Crisis • ALLWECANSAVE.EARTH

All We Can Save, 2019 (One World Books) is an anthology of essays, poems and art by women climate leaders, edited by Dr Ayana Eliza Johnson and Dr Katharine Wilkinson; Kate Orff was one of 60 contributors. It has gone on to create a non-profit organisation providing support and community for women climate leaders.

1   https://www.youtube.com/watch?v=I3vAVhaIElk&feature=emb_title.

2   https://www.youtube.com/watch?v=gkQ4DBvjXw8&feature=emb_title.

Landscapes are Messy and Very, Very Hard Work

Landscape architects have spent decades trying to catch up with architects' visual culture. We sharpen our Illustrator drawings, Photoshop™ ourselves into a corner of perfection and pizzaz. We hire photographers to create passive, pastoral images of swooping meadows and dew-kissed lawns. This is marketing, not reality. Landscapes are labour. By smoothing and polishing our representations of the "ideal" landscape, we leapfrog over what really *makes* them: groups of people working together, doing the hard work of digging, planting, weeding, picking up plastic and debris, pruning, sowing, trimming and sweeping. How can landscape architects represent, photograph, draw and sketch in order to foreground this labour? How do we keep the hand of the land steward in the frame?

152 Kate Orff (SCAPE)
→ New York, NY, USA

103rd Street Community Garden:
Park Raising, New York City, NY, USA
In collaboration with the New York Restoration Project,
SCAPE participated in a "park-raising day" for the 103rd

Street Community Garden in East Harlem – the project
was built on a limited budget, almost entirely with the
help of volunteers.

Design is Falling in Love

For me the design process is like falling in love (with a site). What is unique, special and hidden? How do you foster connections between people and their immediate environs? Site design is an exhausting process – one that requires both emotional and technical investment. Rather than the pursuit of endless novelty, akin to Dali's "paranoid-critical method", I propose a design method that patterns itself after falling in love. Let's foreground passion, creativity and connection in our work and understand that as we plough through technical-drawing sets, everything landscape architects do is a form of loving the Earth and all the species on and below its surface. For every project, I swoon with land-philia.

153 Kate Orff (SCAPE)
→ New York, NY, USA

Toward an Urban Ecology,
New York City, NY, USA, 2016
Oyster gardening in New York Harbor

Follow the Water

A first step in designing landscapes is to study where and how water flows in them. Wherever you follow the water, it tells a story: the history of the land, of displacement, of ownership, power and control. A site's ecological health and social vibrancy tie back to how water is regarded, re-directed, activated and valued – or not. Landscape architects are not trained as policymakers, politicians, historians or anthropologists, but the political and social histories of water can help us forge connections and mend fractured landscapes. As designers, we can learn about land history by looking at hydrology, translating its processes into spatial design and physical landscapes that connect, restore and inspire.

154

Kate Orff (SCAPE)
→ New York, NY, USA

First Avenue Water Plaza, New York City, NY, USA
At the base of the American Copper Buildings along the East River, First Avenue Water Plaza is undergirded by a high-performance water-management system designed by SCAPE to respond to both storms and coastal flood risk.

Excel at Excel

SCAPE represents an ethos, a stance, a collaborative and creative design practice *and* a 75-person mid-sized business with payroll, insurance and complex financial projections. I never imagined that being a business owner would be one of the most exciting and intellectually engaging things I would do in my life, or that I would enjoy the business aspect of practice as much as its creative and design facets. Hand sketching, yes! AutoCAD, yes! Grasshopper software, yes! But the real skill to learn in leadership is how to orchestrate and manage teams and finances through tracking hours and cost over time. It may seem basic, but the software to learn is Microsoft Excel.

(155) Kate Orff (SCAPE)
→ New York, NY, USA

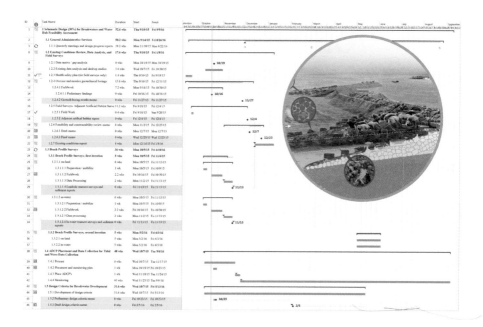

Living Breakwaters design and implementation, Staten Island, NY, USA

Behind the public-facing renderings of every project there are projections and extensive details mapped out in that most basic of tools: Excel. These include Living Breakwaters, SCAPE's proposal for a series of near-shore breakwaters off the southern coast of Staten Island.

5th Façade = 24/7 Landscape

Although the physical constraints brought by a pandemic are only temporary, they are a sharp reminder of the immense value that lies in public accessibility and free movement through urban spaces: an outdoor picnic with good friends, a walk to take in art and fresh air, large masses of people gathering for a concert or finding the perfect spot to watch the sun set. We typically need different, programmed areas of a city in order to have these experiences – parks, galleries, concert halls and terraces. The Norwegian National Opera and Ballet, however, facilitates it all on its roof as a non-programmed space. As a fifth façade the roof is no longer part of a building with opening hours but an urban plaza for the people. Through close collaboration between architects and landscape architects, we seamlessly integrate buildings into our landscapes, and landscapes into our buildings – for everyone to enjoy.

156

Jenny B. Osuldsen (Snøhetta)
→ Oslo, Norway

Norwegian National Opera and Ballet,
Oslo, Norway, 2008

Since its inauguration in 2008 more than 1.7 million people have annually crossed the bridge leading to the
Norwegian National Opera and Ballet – most of them
to take a stroll on the roof, which has led people to refer
to "the Opera roof" as a *place*. The 19,000-square-metre
white Carrara marble jigsaw puzzle consists of 33,000
individual stone pieces, and was created by an interdisciplinary team incorporating three artists, an architect and a landscape architect.

Combine Digital and Analogue Discoveries

For every tool you learn to use, whether analogue or digital, new possibilities appear. It is easy to get carried away, letting the tool's functionality dictate the outcome. We should, rather, let the possibilities discovered set the course. Parametric design was one such discovery in the development of the landscape design for Max IV, a research park in Lund, Sweden. It played a crucial role in the design of an undulating landscape that reduced ground vibration from the nearby highway, allowing the research laboratory to operate with higher accuracy. Equally important, however, were the analogue discoveries. The existing monoculture landscape was transformed into meadowland, essential to improving the area's biodiversity, using analogue methods to harvest meadowland species and letting sheep do the "maintenance". The precise yet rough clay terrain surrounding the Max IV research park was executed using a bulldozer as a live 1:1 3D-plotter on site. Since the opening, researchers have found that ground vibrations caused by the nearby highway have been reduced by 30%, mainly due to the undulating landscape.

157 Jenny B. Osuldsen (Snøhetta)
→ Oslo, Norway

Max IV Laboratory Landscape, Lund, Sweden, 2016
The hay that was sprayed over the mounds was harvested from the neighbouring nature reserve in order to secure a natural selection of meadowland species from the area. Wildlife, in the form of birds and insects, is now reoccupying the open landscape and the "hairy" mounds are the area's new signature, which also invites humans as visitors into the wavy, iconic landscape.

Make Slow Spaces in Urban Jungles

Times Square was once one of the busiest and traffic dominated areas in the world. New Yorkers themselves hated it. Once you were in, getting out was difficult. A trap, they said. The narrow, overcrowded sidewalks forced pedestrians to spill into the roadways. It is still one of the busiest places, but something has changed. Cars were removed, and pedestrians were given access. By almost doubling the pedestrian area, subtle changes such as the elimination of kerbs, the removal of site clutter and the introduction of a street carpet with sculpted horizontal "obelisks" made eye height important and guaranteed a feeling of being safe, as if walking along a building. There are places to sit, walk, talk – to do yoga or meet an old friend. By bringing human scale to an otherwise gargantuan spot on Manhattan Island, the new Times Square became a hotspot from which to experience the beauty of the urban jungle, enjoying people-watching and being singular in the plural at your own pace.

(158) Jenny B. Osuldsen (Snøhetta)
→ Oslo, Norway

Times Square Reconstruction, New York City,
NY, USA, 2016
After closing Broadway to vehicle traffic into New York's
Times Square, pedestrian injuries fell by 40% in the
area[1] despite a 59% increase in pedestrian foot traffic.[2] Almost 80% of visitors say they feel that the new
pedestrian plazas make Times Square a safer, nicer
and a more New York-place to be.[3]

1   Wilson, M. (2015). "Amid Times Square's Bright
Lights, Murders in the Shadows", *New York Times*,
23 January.

2   New York State Department of Transportation
(2014). "Friendlier Broadway Paves Way to Safety in
New York", April.

3   Times Square Alliance (2015). "Roadmap for a
21st Century Times Square", 8 October.

Microscale Landscapes in Urban Backyards

Through an initiative in the 1970s, Oslo's worn-out housing areas from the 1890s were saved from remediation, and their backyards were also given a chance of a new life as politicians allocated resources to urban renewal by means of retaining and restoring. These otherwise lifeless, left-over, in-between spaces were transformed into lush, social meeting points with lasting qualities. This allowed for improvements, in both social sustainability and urban ecology, in these microscale spaces. From 1980 to 2005 more than 300 backyards in downtown Oslo were transformed into meeting places for neighbours. Citizens could apply for funding to cover up to 80% of the cost involved, using professional landscape architects to execute the design and user participation processes. But more importantly, the yards were converted into shared space both for residents to continue to live in the city centre and for visitors to enjoy – an initiative for public health as much as for biodiversity.

(159) Jenny B. Osuldsen (Snøhetta)
→ Oslo, Norway

Oslo's Backyards, revitalised as urban gardens,
Oslo, Norway
This backyard was transformed, using urban ecology and sustainability parameters, from an outworn asphalt-covered area with three car-parking spaces and neglected vegetation to a meeting place for neighbours. The white in-situ concrete with recycled glass creates a *catwalk* through the new urban garden, with white permeable gravel covering a detention basin taking care of surface water. Green frames of perennials and cut hedges of beechwood; ivy as green "fur" on walls; and four small red mirrors, along with custom-made benches, tables and loose chairs, create a comfortable, peaceful and inviting courtyard.

A Long-Term Plan with Invaluable Impact for Generations

Landscape architecture requires patience. More often than not, projects need time to grow into their full potential and originally intended vision. Like its projects, the profession of landscape architecture is itself also a phenomenon of long lines. Already by 1919, Norway was among the first European countries to offer Landscape Architecture as an academic discipline. Its century-long investment in educating landscape architects has resulted in significant long-term planning to secure the establishment, resurgence and protection of urban green spaces and the design of new common landscapes. In 2019 this development was explored in a book about the Norwegian pioneers in landscape architecture and an exhibition at the Norwegian National Museum of Art, Architecture and Design. Being the museum's first ever exhibition on landscape architecture, a century after the profession's manifestation through the country's educational system, it underlines the fact that it is worth waiting for a tree to turn 100 but that you shouldn't forget to take a photo when it is newly planted.

160   Jenny B. Osuldsen (Snøhetta)
→ Oslo, Norway

OUTDOOR VOICES

THE PIONEER ERA OF NORWEGIAN LANDSCAPE ARCHITECTURE

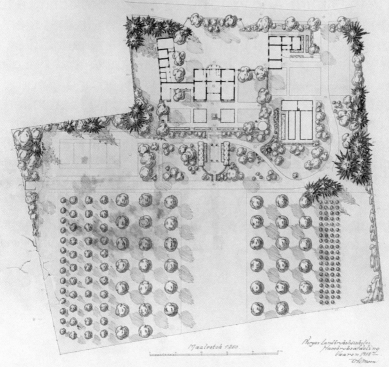

ORFEUS

Outdoor Voices, 2019
The historical archives of Norwegian landscape architecture are managed and maintained by a research group at the School of Landscape Architecture and the University of Life Sciences at Ås, Norway. In 2019 the book *Outdoor Voices* was published to celebrate the pioneering era of the discipline, based on treasures from the archives. Its main purpose was to tell stories to inspire and strengthen research into the history of landscape architecture and green-heritage management. It is about learning from history, taking action today, and all the while thinking of the future.

The Language of Plants is Growth

Plants are the miracle of landscape-architectural design because their very nature is constant change. When we imagine, say, a forest or a tree-lined boulevard we are actually imagining not the material – the tree – now but long in the future. And in doing so we are projecting a future that is consistent and not catastrophic. In that mental picture of the future a protagonist is lurking just out of the frame: the gardener. Intuitively we know that the gardener is there, keeping the plants watered and cared for, yet we don't imagine that this act of care is an inherent part of those plants' materiality, which is not green but made of growth itself. I have devised the term *viridic*,[1] like the concept of *tectonic* in architecture, to recognise that plants need to be celebrated as a unique, transformative material with acts of care at their heart. This challenges landscape architects to practise in real time, not only with drawings.

161

Julian Raxworthy
→ Canberra, ACT, Australia

The pollarding of trees at Insel Hombroich (western Germany) shows how, through a process of "traumatic reiteration", growth is catalysed to make landscape form.

1   Raxworthy, Julian (2018). *Overgrown: Practices between Landscape Architecture and Gardening*. Cambridge, MA: MIT Press, p. 135.

Ownership Shapes the Boundary, but Shouldn't

Ian McHarg taught us to look at the large-scale landscape and see its layers[1] while Richard T. T. Forman helped us to read its patterns, as a mosaic.[2] In the 20th century these types of readings tied landscape architecture to the region – to understanding landscape writ large, which was supposed to help contextualise and inform site design decisions on a smaller scale. That scale was the scale of land tenure and property ownership – because in capitalism there is no landscape that is ambiguous or outside a spatial schema of land value defined through precise surveying techniques that describe exact dimensions of land in drawings and then tie them to contracts in words. The implications of land tenure are to be found in every formal, and thereby spatial, type of landscape architecture: the street? The gap between property boundaries; the park? A certain scale of governmental ownership; a row of trees? The demarcation of a boundary using other means.

162

Julian Raxworthy
→ Canberra, ACT, Australia

The historic coastline of Fremantle, WA, Australia is shown in paving – its fluidity juxtaposed against the arbitrary boundaries of land ownership, manifest in its adjacent kerb.

1   McHarg, Ian L. (1969). *Design with Nature.* New York: Natural History Press.

2   Forman, Richard T. T. (1995). *Land Mosaics: The Ecology of Landscapes and Regions.* Cambridge, UK: Cambridge University Press.

Policy is Design by Other Means

Landscape architecture's responsibility to the time-scale of landscape systems resists the summative limitations of the static drawing. Treating design as a way of thinking allows for speculation in other media better suited to time, like the indexing of maps to building policies and codes, activated later by proposed changes in applications. As Michael Sorkin showed in *Local Codes*,[1] bringing creativity – even humour – to the banal documents of government can mitigate the limitations of both the drawings of designers and the texts of planners. Landscape architecture, because of the way it sits between these acts and the different scales of design, can work in other media, squeezing through gaps in professions to design not just objects but methods – and, thereby, engage with a scale that is unique to the discipline.

(163) Julian Raxworthy
→ Canberra, ACT, Australia

West 8 established urban rules at Borneo Sporenburg, Amsterdam, that constrained the "bounding box" of urban form while allowing for much differentiation, by designers, between dwellings.

1   Sorkin, Michael (1993). *Local Codes*. Cambridge, MA: MIT Press.

The Stick in the Sand

Landscapes often work abstractly, with one thing (an object, for example) creating the conditions for another thing to occur. This is because objects interact with diverse systems in the landscape, becoming catalysts. To design with this approach in mind is to "work at a distance", to do something in order to do something else. Roel van Gerwen has used the analogy of "the stick in the sand" to describe this process.[1] Gerwen contrasts two approaches to making a sandcastle. One is to form it as precisely as possible in sand; however, its form will disappear when faced with the elements of the seaside. The other, for which he argues, locates a stick in the sand and those same forces of wind and sand deposition will cause a "sandcastle-like" form to arise over time. Here, the design and positioning of the stick would be the relevant instruments for orchestrating this emerging form.

164 Julian Raxworthy
→ Canberra, ACT, Australia

The form of posts and sand fencing at a beach creates very specific dynamics in relation to local wind and site conditions, with successive waves of building up and then excavating again.

1   Gerwen, Roel van (2004). "Force Fields in the Daily Practice of a Dutch Landscape Architect", in Julian Raxworthy and Jessica Blood (eds.). *The MESH Book: Infrastructure/Landscape*. Melbourne: RMIT Press, p. 239.

The Ground is Wedged between Sky and Stone

"Water runs downhill" seems like the most banal of reminders but its truth is most visible in what it does to the landscape. Sandwiched between the ever-present turmoil of the sky – sucking up moisture from evapotranspiration here, dumping it as rain there – and the slow churn of millennial geomorphology, erosion shapes topography in a symphony of ridges and valleys. Now – in the city – hyper-precise surfaces are simulations of that process in paving that play by the same rules; minute ridges and almost-invisible valleys mimic larger landscape/geomorphological systems as the designed landscape creates technological analogues. Learning that when a landscape architect looks at a surface that is solid, relentless, they are really simulating its opposite in their mind – ephemeral water, moving across it – is the kind of subtle shift in mindset that characterises our profession.

165 Julian Raxworthy
→ Canberra, ACT, Australia

In this garden by Franchesca Watson for a building by
StudioMAS at the base of Table Mountain, Cape Town,
South Africa, the ground is a thin layer between granite
and the misty atmosphere.

Landscape is Catalytic

No mere background or scenography, landscapes are active environs of work, doing, being. Always in the process of making or unmaking, they can themselves *instigate* response and change.

Consider the act of gently tilting the ground, and how that simple move sheds water towards lower elevations – perhaps, in turn, creating high/dry and low/wet regimes for cultivation and growth. Further manipulating the ground into undulations inaugurates a different set of hydrological and ecological potentials (puddles, vernal pools, wetlands etc.), or – in combination with surfacing in a spongy material like rubber – encourages playful responses and exploration in people, especially children, who are eager to explore the physical and sentient world before them. Consider, too, human and ecological responses in relation to level ground covered by lawn or sand, or steeper rugged mountainside topographies – each of which propels different kinds of action and activity. Scaled-up, designed landscapes have the capacity for positive and transformative change in cities, can clean water and heal the environment, moderate temperature and transform leaf cover, and positively impact on people's everyday lives.

In all these ways, at multiple scales, landscape is active, transformative and catalytic. Leverage these qualities.

166

Chris Reed (STOSS)
→ Boston, MA, USA

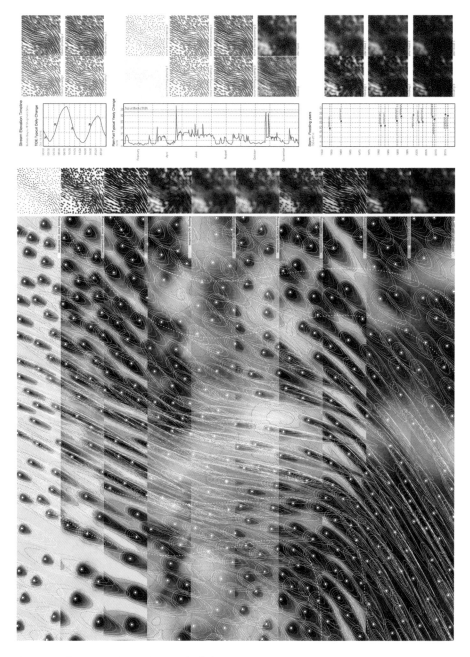

Xun Liu and Ziwei Zhang, *Fluid projections*, for Re-Tooling Metropolis studio; Chris Reed instructor, Harvard Graduate School of Design, 2016.

Embrace Change / Anticipate + Adapt

We know trees, plants and other living things grow. But the entire world is changing, sometimes dramatically, before our eyes. Oceans and rivers rise and fall, and occasionally flood. Weather intensifies and ebbs. Cliffs erode while beaches are built and rebuilt. These are constant, open cycles; conditions do not simply repeat. These open cycles, and the landscapes caught up in them, *evolve* and *adapt*. Odum's Energy Diagram: Energy and Matter Flows through an Ecosystem[1] expresses the open-ended nature of ecosystem dynamics, with inputs and outputs that connect a particular ecosystem to external forces – forces that could shape and be shaped by internal forces and mechanisms. Models like Odum's partly inform complex adaptive systems ecology, which explicitly acknowledges that environmental health is best measured by an organism's or an ecosystem's ability not merely to survive or even resist change in the environment, but especially to adapt to it.

The inevitability of change in landscapes and cities is a powerful and necessary frame for strategy and design. Our thinking and work should anticipate and adapt – remain open both to changes and dynamics we know and, perhaps counterintuitively, to those we cannot know.

(167) Chris Reed (STOSS)
→ Boston, MA, USA

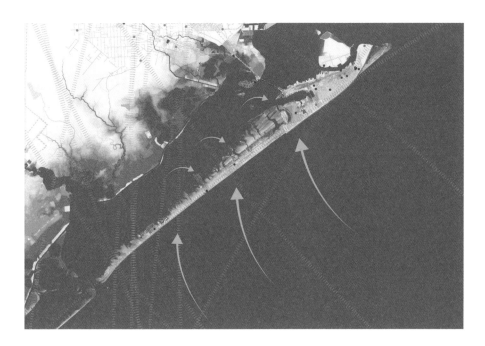

Barrier island dynamics, Galveston Island, TX, USA

1   Odum, Howard T. (1971). *Environment, Power, and Society*. New York: Wiley-Interscience.

Render the Invisible Visible / Amplify the Muted

So many sites – urbanised or previously occupied ones especially – have many things to hide, many things to unearth, many things to discover. Industrial and urban developments typically obliterate ecological functions and environmental dynamics. Histories are buried – including those of early inhabitants and Indigenous populations who lived lightly on the land; and often including Black and other racial or ethnic minorities whose neighbourhoods were deliberately eliminated by racist violence and planning, zoning and urban-renewal activities.

There is a richness here to be mined – not to be replicated but to be brought to light, reinitiated, remembered, honoured and reinvested in, in new and meaningful ways. Embodied, denuded and buried histories, cultures, environmental dynamics and people can be surfaced as design "informants" – at multiple scales. Importantly, these latent and buried pasts can broaden the starting points for design; can help to reverse deliberate (and not-so-deliberate) processes and policies that have oppressed and muted a fuller and more diverse set of inhabitants and actors in the landscape; and can put us on a path towards creating more inclusive, more healthful, more grounded and more beautiful landscapes and open spaces.

168 Chris Reed (STOSS)
→ Boston, MA, USA

Unearthing BIPOC (Black, Indigenous and People
of Colour) histories, St Louis, MO, USA

Landscape is a Cultural Project

Landscape can do many things – cleanse water, air and soil; cool down cities and improve public health; transform the nature of cities and urban life; have remediative environmental effects; and reverse long-standing social and environmental injustices.

Designing landscape, though, is fundamentally a projective, imaginative and creative act. Like fine arts and architecture, landscape architecture is a *cultural* project – one that just happens to embrace the living world. In this vein, develop a set of design agendas – avenues of exploration and elaboration – and let this work inform your design thinking broadly (not just in solving problems). Investigate colour, texture and materiality; figure, form and qualities of the field; landform and earth; structure and accommodation.

For, truthfully, we are not better environmentalists or social scientists than trained environmentalists and social scientists themselves; we are not better activists than full-time activists. We will never be those things, though these agendas can and should form important parts of our work. Rather, our distinction as a discipline lies in our integrative and projective capacities, in our larger cultural (design) project – the Project *behind* our projects.[1] And our collective voice – our cultural capital – depends on this.

169) Chris Reed (STOSS)
→ Boston, MA, USA

Robert Rauschenberg, *Estate*, Photomontage, oil and screenprinted inks on canvas, 1963. Gift of the Friends of the Philadelphia Museum of Art, 1967.

1   This idea is an extension of a series of conversations with Julia Czerniak, captured in her essay "Appearance and (Aesthetic) Experience: The Ongoing Project of Stoss", in Chris Reed and Mike Belleme (2021). *Mise-en-Scène: The Lives and Afterlives of Urban Landscapes.* Novato, CA: ORO Editions.

Design for Life

Design for fun, for play, for the everyday. Design for quietude, and for intimate moments. Design for individual and collective joy, and outrage, and sadness, and hope. Design for the mundane, the extraordinary and the peculiar.

Design for all the things we do, for all the things plants and animals and ecosystems do, and for all the things that infrastructures and cities do and can do.

170 Chris Reed (STOSS)
→ Boston, MA, USA

Parade in downtown St Louis, MO, USA

Superficial Surfaces

While architects concern themselves with the inside as a different entity from the outside – even though they sometimes attempt to overcome this dichotomy – landscape architects don't follow this distinction. For us there exists a different sensitivity regarding surfaces, for the thin layer between earth and sky makes up our canvas. By means of form giving and graphical treatment we can activate such surfaces, so that our ideas find a place where they become tangible and visually comprehensible. Surfaces are the central starting point of our work process as landscape architects, and they demand an understanding of the definition and clarification of the expanse of the terrain in question. In the Maselake Canal project, graphic designs installed on the former industrial site explore this interpretation of surfaces in landscape architecture. Users are encouraged to interpret the site as they wish and engage with it accordingly, creating personal experiences of the space.

171

Martin Rein-Cano (Topotek 1)
→ Berlin, Germany

Maselake Canal project, Berlin, Germany, 2006
Playful pattern on the asphalt ground in Spandau, along
with yellow and black dividers, reference the site's industrial history. Designers: Topotek 1

The Fetish of Things

The objects in our urban spaces – furniture, plants, trees etc. – are subject to individual interpretation while carrying the designer's intended identity. Attached to these objects, therefore, is an emotionalisation and attraction that, upon further development, can give public open spaces a strong character and allure. Depending on the context of these objects are, this subjectivity may be turned into a desired fetishisation. This design strategy, of transforming an object in such a way that it generates a power of attraction, awards the space that the object occupies a desired design quality. For designers, an understanding and belief in the fetishising of things will empower them to turn a banal object into an animated one. As such, fetishisation – an excessive devotion – will give agency to an object like a dentist's sign, creating a new identity in a new context. Its characteristics are expanded by the space and its people, as it is able to take on new interpretations.

172 Martin Rein-Cano (Topotek 1)
→ Berlin, Germany

Superkilen, Copenhagen, Denmark, 2012
A dentist's sign in the middle of the Black Market, doing
everything except signalling a dentist's surgery.
Designers: Topotek 1, BIG and SUPERFLEX

Being and Staying Foreign

Even today inspiration is still taken from the traditional English landscape garden, and objects are accordingly imported from all around the world in order to create spaces of great character in our urban landscape. Intimately connected with these translocations is the notion of "foreignness", guiding the progression of including and moving various artefacts. Once taken out of their original context, all artefacts – and also, more conceptually, all ideas – undergo change to some extent. A necessary side effect of such translocation is therefore translation – and the possibility that, as Jorge Luis Borges put it, "[t]he original is unfaithful to the translation."[1] Even though those artefacts have been transformed, they will remain foreign in their new context. The newly created spaces gain much of their character from such fundamental foreignness.

(173) Martin Rein-Cano (Topotek 1)
→ Berlin, Germany

Picturesque foreignness
The Palladian bridge with the Pantheon in the background at the Stourhead estate in Wiltshire, UK.

1   Borges, Jorge Luis (1999). "On William Beckford's
Vathek", in Jorge Luis Borges. *Selected Non-Fictions*.
New York: Penguin Putnam Inc., pp. 236–239.

Cultivating Conflicts

Conflicts carry with them a negative connotation in everyday life, but in our profession they are the gateway to creative interactions. The transformation of such conflicts is initiated by allowing a clash of aesthetics as well as various forms of appropriation of functions and usages in order to reach a maximum level of creative, often surprising, possibilities. Instead of turning a blind eye to existing conflicts in the hope that they will resolve themselves, one should embrace them since they are a real part of everyday life and cannot, and should not, be covered up. Acknowledging the reality of places will ultimately lead to a multifaceted public open space. Creating spatial and aesthetic settings in which conflicts can be expressed will transform them into productive, creative interactions. We will find ourselves with complex spaces that have a strong character, and we'll avoid a numb, muted-down space.

174

Martin Rein-Cano (Topotek 1)
→ Berlin, Germany

Wasserpicknick, Federal Horticultural Show,
Schwerin, Germany, 2009
A purposefully conflicting situation in Schwerin: picnic
tables placed in the water create a unique spatial experience.

Fail Better

While failure is unavoidable in our occupation, over time you learn to overcome and, more importantly, to channel and transform it. In my years as a landscape architect, I've learned that we must train ourselves to fail and to do so in a way that realises the actual components of failure – not overlooking them by focusing on a euphemistic, idealised outcome. Samuel Beckett put this notion into words best: "Try again. Fail again. Fail better."[1] Losing a competition or plummeting into a creative black hole are realities for every landscape architect, and they should be treated as such. It is tough situations that take our creativity to the next level and force us to reflect on and understand what can be improved in future projects. Only when accepting the brutal reality of failing can we move forward in order to brace ourselves for the next, slightly less dramatic, failure.

(175) Martin Rein-Cano (Topotek 1)
→ Berlin, Germany

Shot from Stanley Kubrick's 2001:
A Space Odyssey (1968)
Setting off on new quests again and again, acknowledging and transforming obstacles along the way – as
demonstrated in the classic science-fiction movie.

1   Beckett, Samuel (1983). *Worstward Ho.* New York:
Grove Press.

The Expanded Context of Land over 12,000 Years

In Canada we are designing upon land with at least 12,000 years of continuous inhabitation – most of it unceded, traditional territory of the First Nations, Inuit and Métis peoples. That is the expanded context – we need the humility and flexibility to work within it. This means both learning and unlearning as we adapt the way we practise. More than ever we are profoundly open to new forms of collaboration, listening to those who knew a place first. The insights are humbling and often call into question our professional tools for "solving" or "envisioning". Working in this expanded context can't be about definitive answers; rather, it's a search for the *source* for answers, and the start of posing challenging new questions. We are not the authors of a site, but the next generation seeking deeper connections with a place and its long histories and ecologies – seeking enduring dialogues in order to shape new futures.

176   Marc Ryan (PUBLIC WORK)
→ Toronto, ON, Canada

Nepean Point, Ottawa, ON, Canada, 2017
How can landscape architects advance change within this expanded context? And how do we ensure our solutions aren't defined or prescribed by normative standards? Could a park-making process be a spatial response to the process of reconciliation – a platform for dialogue and coming together? In contrast to the picturesque parks of the capital, Nepean Point was a provocative proposal for a new kind of park – one that creates both space and time for the Indigenous community to lead the collaborative discovery of what a gathering space for all Canadians could be.

Our Work is Never Finished

It takes a different orientation to embrace the design of places that sustain the dynamics of constant evolution – rather than fixed compositions – but it's at the core of what is so amazing about landscape. We try to apply fundamental landscape sensibilities to the design of urban places, layering these process-based qualities into the design of the public realm and, in turn, the way in which public life is cultivated. Cities endure and remain relevant precisely because they are constantly changing. It's so refreshing to encounter designed places that aren't in an end state: spaces in which people are invited to be active participants in shaping how they feel and evolve over time. If public spaces in cities are deliberately conceived as forever in progress, we get closer to spaces that feel spontaneous, that remain open, leaving space for others to add their "fingerprints" and inspire new action. This understanding can be at once practical, adaptive and symbolic, and – hopefully – produce memorable and engaging places.

(177) Marc Ryan (PUBLIC WORK)
→ Toronto, ON, Canada

National Holocaust Monument Competition,
Ottawa, ON, Canada, 2014
When collaborating on this monument with Wodiczko +
Bonder, we were guided by James E. Young's thinking
that only an *unfinished* memorial process can guaran-
tee the life of memory. Our proposed "working monument" is also living; it's a slowly unfolding environment
that engages both human action (ongoing rituals of
adding and inter-mixing soils) and ecological processes (weathering of incisions in bedrock, growth of aspen
grove) for it to thrive. We have found this way of thinking to be a relevant model for the design of the public
realm in cities.

Resourcefulness

When living and working in Tirana, Albania in the early 2000s I saw the intelligence of a so-called developing nation that was way ahead of anything I was familiar with in terms of its ingenuity in reimagining a city under pressure. I was forever changed. This inspired an ongoing pursuit of impactful design interventions using the most minimal means possible. An ethos of resourcefulness can express itself at every scale – from the selection of materials through to individual sites, urban infrastructure and even at the scale of the city as a whole. For me, it opened up a way of looking at our existing cityscape in search of opportunities for transformation and impact – by recasting existing resources rather than covering up or starting over. Leveraging what came before and re-situating it as part of a new public realm can lead us to discover urban landscapes of a different kind.

Marc Ryan (PUBLIC WORK)
→ Toronto, ON, Canada

The Bentway, Toronto, ON, Canada, 2018
The starting point for conceptualising The Bentway was the structure itself. The expressway's supportive concrete columns ("bents") create a series of civic rooms that can function collectively or independently to offer spaces for a diverse range of programming and events.

We did as little as possible. The underside of the expressway is recast as a metropolitan-scaled piece of public equipment, while the public spaces and trail stitch together seven neighbourhoods and create a new gathering place for Toronto's growing population.

Be a Local with Fresh Eyes

Home should be the ideal place to practise; it's the place we know best. But over time we can get stuck in a static way of seeing these familiar places or be pulled into the status quo. I practise in the city where I was raised (and then left and returned), so I'm conscious of trying to maintain a fresh outlook on my environment as if both an insider and outsider. I'm also trying to stay attuned to those details (big and small) and particularities about the place – which can either be overlooked or slowly forgotten – and to remember that they are, in fact, remarkable. If we can learn to discover and rediscover our local condition, we can translate that perception to create works that re-awaken a sense of wonder in others about our environment. The ultimate local practice focuses on the familiar with fresh eyes, putting emphasis on the points of strategic impact in the places in which we live and work.

179) Marc Ryan (PUBLIC WORK)
→ Toronto, ON, Canada

TOcore Downtown Parks Vision,
Toronto, ON, Canada, 2018
It helps to maintain a perspective of the whole city in order to make sense of the small, independent sites where we often work. We can then look past the "edges" of conventional plans or client's properties to embrace the larger systems that our profession can weave back into everyday life. Working on a vision for Toronto's downtown parks and public realm allowed us to be both proactive and reactive. It forced us to conceive our local projects within a larger, more coherent idea about the city as a landscape.

"Think Green and Fill Your Work with Love"

This was the last thing Rich Haag told me when I left his Seattle office in 2001. I was young (less than three years into my career) and I wasn't ready to grasp its potency. I might have been so fuelled at the time by a desire to create something "critical" or "new" in landscape that I took his words as being slightly romantic. But they made an impression on me. This was one of the most radical landscape architects I'd ever met... Could it be this simple? It took me years of life and work to find my way to Rich's wisdom and fully appreciate both the simplicity and complexity of his Zen-like way of practising. He has profoundly shaped my outlook and his message still guides me today: recognise the urgency and centrality of the environment in everything you do, and never hesitate to let your passion and optimism drive your work.

180

Marc Ryan (PUBLIC WORK)
→ Toronto, ON, Canada

Gas Works Park, Seattle, WA, USA, 2004
Rich Haag was, for me, a model of the fusion of land-scape architecture and civic activism. Gas Works Park, Seattle, created in the early 1970s, will forever be an inspiration in design perception, persuasion and per-severance as well as a brave, early experiment in landscape remediation and reclamation. Look at this masterwork – it's an ever-relevant example for a new generation of practitioners, reminding us that to innov-ate we need tireless energy and spirit to self-initiate projects and processes able to engage communities as well as being politically minded.

Timefulness

In Roman iconography the *genius* of the place was often depicted as a figure holding a *cornucopia*, a metaphor promising the present-day landscape architect that consults her the rich reward of being able to express the essential identity of the site.[1] But are all the goodies rolling out of this horn of plenty enough to make a successful design? It's a good start, but it is only the *mise en place* of a rich array of spatial characteristics and connotations. We need the programming, boiling, steaming, cooking and assembling processes to shape it into a dish. If something like *the spirit of the place* exists, there must certainly be something like *the spirit of the process*, too.[2] And although landscape architects work with living material, they haven't yet developed a rich vocabulary for processes that accurately characterise their workings, rhythm, amplitude and widely different time scales. To become process-literate, we need to develop timefulness.[3]

181 Dirk Sijmons
→ Amsterdam, The Netherlands

The changing shape of the Sand Engine, from completion to 13 August 2014

"Site" might be where the *genius* of the place meets the *genius* of the process. An artificial dune, aka the Sand Engine (52.054330, 4.187569) supplies sand to the weak parts of the dune coast. The Earth–Moon system (periodicity, some 30 days) causes the North Sea Basin to fill up and drain again. The resulting tides (every six hours) produce a coastal stream (two steps forward, one step back), slowly eroding the Sand Engine (lifespan: 30 years) and transporting sand to sediment along the coast.[4]

1   Kahn, Andrea and Burns, Carol J. (2020). *Site Matters – Strategies for Uncertainty Through Planning and Design*, second edition. Abingdon, UK: Routledge.

2   Sijmons, Dirk (2015). *Moved Movement*. Delft: TU Delft, Faculty of Architecture and the Built Environment.

3   Bjornerud, Marcia (2018). *Timefulness – How Thinking Like a Geologist Can Help Save the World*. Princeton, NJ: Princeton University Press.

4   Stive, Marcel, Luijendijk, Arjen, Ranasinghe, Roshanka et al. (2013). "The Sand Engine: A Solution for Vulnerable Deltas in the 21st Century?" Paper presented at the Conference: Coastal Dynamics 2013, 7th International Conference on Coastal Dynamics, Arcachon, France, 24–28 June.

Reverse Engineering

Looking back, one can't help but observe that the most interesting designs of the last 50 years were almost all brownfield parks.[1] From Parc de la Villette in Paris and Duisburg-Nord in Germany's Ruhr region to New York's High Line, our field has been instrumental in transforming the moraines of the industrial glacier into parks. There might be another formidable task ahead: healing the wounds inflicted by modernist engineering. In urban areas, this repertoire is already beginning to materialise in the conversion of concrete storm drains into green-blue infrastructure that adds public space to the city. Looking at the landscape through this lens reveals a myriad of tasks. Reverse engineering of too-one-sided agricultural water systems, the demolition of obsolete dams in order to restart fish migration, the reconnection of fragmented nature areas – the list goes on. We shouldn't just leave this new frontier to grassroots activists and ecologists. Our discipline must help shape these developments by adding a meaningful cultural layer.[2]

182   Dirk Sijmons
      → Amsterdam, The Netherlands

1   van der Velde, René (2018). "Transformation in Composition – Ecdysis of Landscape Architecture through the Brownfield Park Project 1975–2015", doctoral thesis #09, TU Delft, Faculty of Architecture and the Built Environment.

2   Brugmans, George and Strien, Jolanda (eds.) (2014). *IABR–2014–Urban by Nature*. Catalogue curated by Dirk Sijmons. Rotterdam: International Architecture Biennale Rotterdam Publishers.

3   Belletti, Barbara; Garcia de Leaniz, Carlos; Jones, Joshua et al. (2020). "More than one million barriers fragment Europe's rivers", *Nature* 588; pp. 436–441.

Fatou Dam, Haute-Loire, France
Recent research reveals that there are more than a million barriers of all kinds in European rivers – sluices, locks, culverts, portages, dams, pumping stations, hydropower plants – obstructing fish migration.[3] In France alone, some 7,000 dams of widely varying sizes have become obsolete but funds to remove them are rarely available. The image shows the Fatou Dam on the Beaume River in the upper basin of the Loire: a small hydropower plant erected in 1907, which ceased operation in 1957 and was removed in 2007.

The Necessity of Constant Gardening

The modernist division of labour has created a separation in architecture between design ("we" do that); execution (the contractor does that); and maintenance (painters, window cleaners and maintenance mechanics do that). The last-named are hired to keep the building in pristine condition, as many Modernist buildings do not age gracefully. As landscape architects, we have allowed this separation to happen. Wrongly. Landscape architecture is distinguished by working with living materials and living processes. This often means practising "judo" with ecological succession, favouring certain species and suppressing others to get the desired result. Rewilding is also allowed, if a conscious choice. In short, our profession revolves around the garden and the necessity of constant gardening, and our designs must be allowed to come of age. Patient, repetitive actions create enormous spatial and ecological variation, while, counterintuitively, doing something different each time leads to uniformity.[1] We have to rediscover the formidable formative power of management.

(183) Dirk Sijmons
→ Amsterdam, The Netherlands

Kokedera, Kyoto, Japan: the moss garden
The 14th-century Japanese monk Musō Kokushi founded and laid out the Zen garden Saihoji that was to
become known as "Kokedera", the moss garden.[2] After some decades, the monks observed that mosses
especially thrived there and decided to optimise their
management to account for these modest creatures.
The meticulous removal of twigs, fruits and seedlings
for almost 700 years resulted in a magic garden that
boasts a highly differentiated moss field of just shy
of 120 species, with a corresponding myriad of shades
of green.

1   de Jong, Taeke, de Vries, Ger, Tjallingii, Sybrand
et al. (eds.) (2015). *The Theory of Chris van Leeuwen*.
Delft: TU Delft, Faculty of Architecture and the Built
Environment.

2   Treib, Marc and Herman, Ron (2018). *A Guide to
the Gardens of Kyoto*. San Francisco: ORO Editions.

Take a Holiday from Being Human

As we have to design for non-human earthlings too, the question arises, how we can empathise with the wishes of these additional clients. Shamans and artists have preceded us, mainly focusing on large species that are quite similar to humans.[1] That leaves most of our living planet neglected. Lichens might provide an "entrance ticket" to the dazzling complexity of our biosphere. They arise from the ancient symbiosis between fungi and algae. The fungus provides protection and adhesion, and the algae provide glucose through photosynthesis. With its symbionts from different domains of the tree of life, this interaction was a mystery at first, and has been a nightmare for taxonomists ever since. Recently, specific mixes of bacteria were also found to be part of this life form,[2] which was hitherto considered to be a dual organism. A lichen, however, turns out to be a microbiome: a "get-together" of Earth's most important life forms, a planet on a micro-scale – sublime and literally unidentifiable. Enjoy your vacation!

(184) Dirk Sijmons
→ Amsterdam, The Netherlands

Your friendly neighbourhood lichen
Calogaya decipiens (as it is formally known, showing some of the taxonomic skirmishes inherent in defining this extraordinary life form) is an urbanite and your friendly neighbourhood lichen. It can be found on all kinds of basic rocks and stones, ranging from basalt to concrete to bricks.

1   Foster, Charles (2016). *Being a Beast.* London: Profile Books; and Twaithes, Thomas (2016). *GoatMan: How I Took a Holiday from Being Human.* New York: Princeton Architectural Press.

2   Sheldrake, Merlin (2020). *Entangled Life: How Fungi Make Our Worlds, Change Our Minds & Shape Our Futures.* New York: Random House, p. 106.

Don't Overreach; Don't Underestimate Either

As an echo of 20th-century spatial determinism, some still seem to believe that virtually all social and environmental problems can be solved by spatial means. Maxims like "systemic design can change the world"[1] keep alive the illusion that the world pivots around spatial planning. This type of thinking can lead us to overreach and could seriously erode our credibility, as we cannot deliver on its exaggerated claims.

We have to nurture modesty by acknowledging the limits of our profession. At the same time, we should not underestimate the unique strength of our field. All the important societal challenges we face – from climate adaptation to energy transition, agricultural reform, mobility issues and more – meet each other in the landscape. Design can therefore "build bridges" between widely different practices and shape new syntheses at various scales. This is a task that offers every reason for more legitimate self-confidence, and, as a bonus, a solid base for cooperation with the social and economic disciplines.

185

Dirk Sijmons
→ Amsterdam, The Netherlands

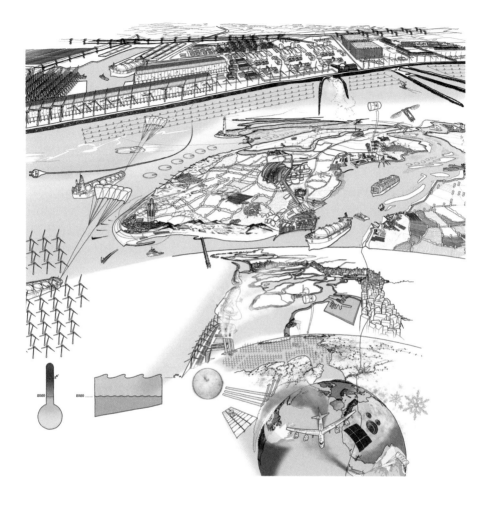

Middle section of a multiscale map of Sloehaven, the Walcheren Peninsula on the Westerschelde, the coast of Zeeland and Holland, northwestern Europe and the English Channel, and the northwestern hemisphere of the globe in the 2134 Eco-modernist scenario.

This scenario postulates a 2.5 degrees warming and 2.0 m sea-level rise, and draws a synthesised picture of the effects and policies of the energy transition, water safety, nature, food supply, the environment and settlement patterns. This is one of four scenarios (Denialist, Eco-modernist, Post-humanist and Anthropocentrism 2.0) from the "Pop Down | Melt Up" study.[2]

1   Berger, Alan (2009). *Systemic Design can Change the World*. Nijmegen: Sun Publishers.

2   *Pop Down | Melt Up. Diepe adaptatie voor een verre toekomst* 2020 [Deep Adaptation to a Remote Future]. Middelburg: CBK Zeeland.

Topography as the Starting Ground

Everything starts with topography. From water runoff to accessibility for all, topography has a major impact on any landscape project. But it should not only be a constraint, it should also become an opportunity. Topography has the power to transform a site. Whereas in nature it is the result of decades of weathering and erosion, in design topography can become the means to create a new landscape. Topography decides where water accumulates, where people prefer to walk and where plants choose to grow.

Topography is about preparing the ground for future life to develop. It surpasses simple, local inclinations as it always is part of a greater geographical entity – part of a valley or part of a mountain. Where architects look for a perfect horizontality to organise the functions required of their buildings, landscape architects should be looking for the ideal undulations to help living communities to thrive. Remember, even the horizon is curved.

186 Bas Smets
→ Brussels, Belgium

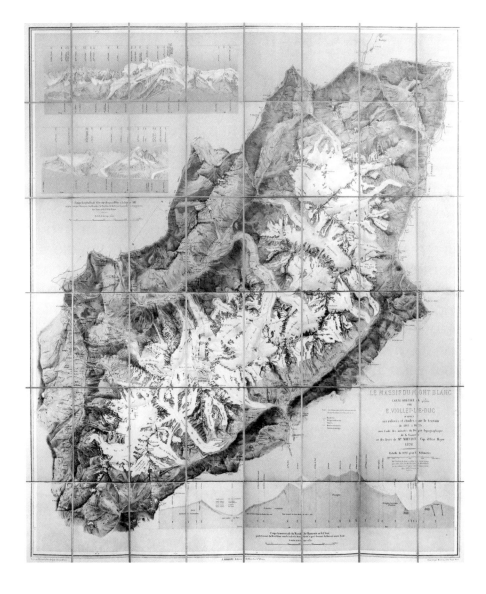

"Le Massif du Mont Blanc", Eugène-Emmanuel Viollet-Le-Duc, 1868–1879

Viollet-Le-Duc is best known for his restorations of France's most prominent churches, among them the Notre-Dame in Paris. He also was a passionate explorer and had studied the Mont Blanc massif for more than a decade. This detailed map is the culmination of a "study of its geodesic and geological construction, of its transformations, and of the… state of its glaciers". For Viollet-Le-Duc there was no essential difference between constructions made by humans and mountains made by nature. Both can be understood and restored if so required.

Understanding Climatic Conditions

The urban context we work in has to be understood as an artificial climate. Buildings change wind patterns and have a direct influence on sun and shading. Roads and pavements interfere with water infiltration and absorb sun-rays, resulting in "heat islands".

The built environment is, by definition, an artificial one. As a result, a city consists of a myriad of microclimatic moments. It is important to understand the climatic condition of a specific site, as it may differ from one street to another. Climate thus becomes a way of designing. Which plants to introduce in this microclimate? Where to position a bench to capture a sunray at noon? How to block the cold wind in winter while still allowing a refreshing breeze in summer? It is important to acknowledge the fact that climate is both a global and a local condition. Both scales should be addressed simultaneously in each project.

187 Bas Smets
→ Brussels, Belgium

Biospheric Urbanism,
Bureau Bas Smets, 2018
Within the expanse of the atmosphere, humankind occupies a thin layer of only several hundred metres of
the Earth's crust. However, this inhabited layer often
creates an impermeable barrier between the air above
and the ground below.

A better understanding of geology will indicate where
and how to infiltrate water, while a better understanding of the climate will allow us to use rainwater, wind
and solar heat as assets. This sectional rendering
explores a "biospheric urbanism" wherein man-made
space becomes the interface between meteorological
effects and geological reality.

Using the Logics of Nature

A landscape project should never merely imitate an image of nature but should always work with the logics of nature. What plants grow where, why and how? A good understanding of climatic conditions is essential for designing a landscape. Similar climatic conditions in a natural situation should be examined in order for nature to become a source of inspiration – not for what it looks like, but for what is possible in terms of plant growth. This research should focus on root development: how much volume is needed, to what minimum depth? The section is more important than the plan as, in landscape architecture, the latter is often the result of the former. This research will allow us to introduce plants into an artificial environment that is strangely similar to their natural habitat. A better understanding of the logics of nature will help to conceive a new urban landscape that can better adapt to our built environment.

188 Bas Smets
→ Brussels, Belgium

GÉOGRAPHIE DES PLANTES ÉQUINOXIALES.

Tableau physique des Andes et Pays voisins

Dressé d'après des Observations & des Mesures prises Sur les lieux depuis le 10.e degré de latitude boréale jusqu'au 10.e de latitude australe en 1799, 1800, 1801, 1802 et 1803.

PAR

ALEXANDRE DE HUMBOLDT ET AIMÉ BONPLAND.

Deposé et relié sous la Nouvelle Académie de Géologie à Anglo-Mexicaine pour les Bayses de Latté par Sarah Legere, per Anglais.

"Géographie des Plantes Équinoxiales",
Alexander von Humboldt, 1805

During his extensive travels to the Americas in the early 19th century Alexander von Humboldt tried to describe everything he encountered. He wanted to understand how nature works as a whole, and sought to combine diverse fields of knowledge into one interconnected entity. This famous section through the Chimborazo Volcano shows all measures taken at different elevations: plant communities, soil cultivation, animal life, air pressure, humidity, temperature and even the blueness of the sky. Considering all these observations simultaneously, Humboldt had an extraordinary capability to extrapolate them into general principles.

Accelerating Ecological Succession

The natural ecological succession of vegetation in a certain area reaches a relative stable state over time. In this process one vegetation community is replaced by another, in a process known as succession, until the climax community is established.

This natural process can be used to bring vegetation back to an abandoned site. Through an intelligent choice of plants, the force driving the ecological succession can be accelerated. Plants from successive communities are planted at the same time in order for one to push the others to grow more quickly. This acceleration can help to rewild an area that has been cleared. Instead of planting mature trees, tapping into the process of succession uses the force of nature to transform a site. This gradual transformation creates a much more resilient vegetation community over time. Instead of imagining the end state of a project, the process by which to reach it becomes the main focus of the design.

(189) Bas Smets
→ Brussels, Belgium

+1.50
+1.20
+0.90
+0.60
+0.45
+0.30
+0.15

Parc des Ateliers, Soil Depth, Arles
Bureau Bas Smets, 2018
The recolonisation by plants of an abandoned industrial site in Arles is conceived as an accelerated process of plant succession. Dunes of fertile soil are installed on its concrete platform, as if they had been blown there over time by prevailing winds.

This diagrammatic section shows how the depth of the soil defines the plant type. Starting with the pioneer plants on the shallowest soil, each increase in soil depth corresponds with a successive plant community.

The movement through space along the dune thus becomes a movement through time, radically transforming the space/time notion.

Urbanism of the Underground

Most cities have been built close to available fertile ground. Over time their expansion has impermeabilised these fields with roads and buildings. Gradually "the underground" has been filled up with services, from sewers to gas, electricity and subway tunnels. This has usually been done without a general plan or idea.

Today it is impossible to obtain a clear view of what lies underneath pavements and plazas. There is an urgent need for a precise cartography of the underground. Based on this mapping an "Urbanism of the Underground" can be developed. This will allow us to understand better where space can be found to provide fertile soil in which trees can grow. The opening around the trunks will allow rainwater to infiltrate below. Runoff is thus stored where it falls, right beneath the pavement. It is reinjected into the air through the transpiration of the trees, lowering the air temperature in the process.

190

Bas Smets
→ Brussels, Belgium

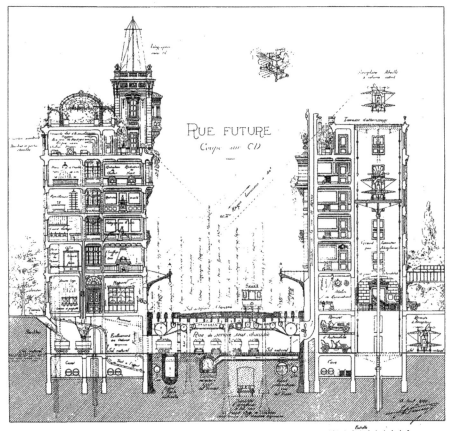

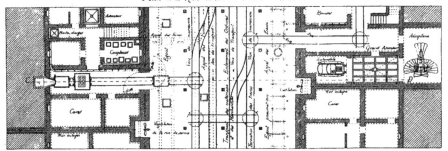

Cities of the Future,
Eugène Hénard, 1910

A century ago, Eugène Hénard was already complaining about the lack of organisation of below-ground services: "All these pipes and tubes are located above or beside one another without order or method. When they have to be repaired, each system … has to be dealt with separately, without any co-operative plan, and as occasion arises."

In his well-known sectional rendering of the future street, Hénard argued it should be designed as a multi-layered construction, like the adjacent buildings. To this day his "coupe" still shows the urgency of reinventing the street.

Drawing is a Sacred Act

The implements you use to birth your vision into the world are an extension of yourself, therefore they deserve careful consideration. If you don't have one already, get yourself a good fountain pen. Head down to your local art store or pen shop and check out their inventory.

Always keep your sketchbook within reach, with your pen ready to observe and record what you see. Build up a reservoir of ideas. I use sketchbooks in a variety of sizes. Find one that is convenient to carry and that is compatible with your drawing style. If it is too cumbersome to access you will be less inclined to use it. Remember, every spare moment is an opportunity to draw – and with every mark you make in this sacramental process, you embark on a quest for creative expression.

191

Chip Sullivan
→ Berkeley, CA, USA

Draw every day! Your sketchbook and pen are your passports into a parallel dimension. Every blank page in your sketchbook is an opportunity for visual adventure, a portal for investigation and experimentation. Your imagination becomes alive in your sketchbook; dance through your visions with your pen. Capture those fleeting moments of insight, or they will vanish and be lost forever.

The *Genius Loci*

Never forget to consult the *genius loci*, or spirit of a place. It is the foundation of our profession. Every location has a distinct spirit of place. The principle dates back to the Ancient Greeks and Romans, who erected shrines and temples to the *genii* that inhabited each unique landscape. In order to grasp the *genius loci* at the renowned Sea Ranch site in northern California, esteemed landscape architect Lawrence Halprin camped out for a week to analyse the place before he began his design. Experience the landscape first-hand. Our reliance on digital techniques moves us further and further away from direct observation of the landscapes we are designing and inhabiting.

Chip Sullivan
→ Berkeley, CA, USA

The landscape is alive; it is a living, breathing entity. Can you find the spirits of place that reside in the landscape? Take a moment and look through the above image. Wander around the woods. Look again! The *genius loci* is waiting to be discovered. Attune yourself to the rhythms of nature, the hidden characteristics that can't be found at a first glance. Only through a sustained period of observation can you catch the transitory moods, rhythms and cycles of nature.

Understand the Fundamentals of Climate Design

Where is the sun? Know the yearly cycle of the sun's movement, and design for proper solar orientation. Create solar pockets and spaces that take advantage of the sun's warmth during the cool seasons. What is the direction of the prevailing winds throughout the year? Funnel the cooling summer breezes into your garden's structures and habitats with vegetation. In the winter, block the cold northern winds with densely planted hedgerows. Incorporate water features that act as passive air-conditioning by aerating the water to cool the air. Be knowledgeable about the climate in the context of future conditions as well as current patterns. Using its historical vocabulary, landscape design has unlimited potential to reduce energy consumption and become the foundation of a green future. Many new and exciting possibilities lie ahead for the creation of garden forms that not only conserve energy but are also works of art and places of spiritual renewal with an intimate connection to the seasons, time and place.

193 Chip Sullivan
→ Berkeley, CA, USA

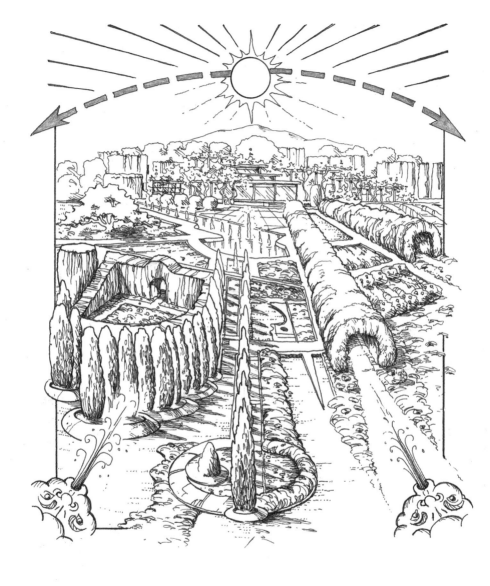

Energy-efficient landscape architecture is still in its infancy. New systems will merge energy conservation with aesthetics. Passive garden design can be both functional and beautiful.

Do the Coolest Thing Ever!

Be self-motivated to pursue your personal interests and passions. No one is going to give you your dream project. You must be self-directed, determined and dedicated in order to cultivate your creativity. Innovation must come from within; you can't wait for the perfect project to come your way. Establish a consistent, sacrosanct time and a personal workspace in which to work. Power off your mobile phone and wifi when you are working. Don't let anything interfere with this time, no matter how hard the temptation might be to head down to the pub with friends. Work first, then reward yourself with that beer. Aim to work on three different projects at the same time. Accept that your ideas are valuable. Find your passion. What is it that you want to do more than anything else in the world?

194

Chip Sullivan
→ Berkeley, CA, USA

Don't be afraid to "blow it out" and make speculative landscapes that are visionary and provocative. Once you've put together a body of work, get your ideas out into the world. As the great innovators of the past were, be prepared to be criticised and ridiculed. Persevere; continue to exhibit, write and lecture. Search, experiment, explore – and, most of all, communicate.

Become a Mentor

You have the opportunity and the responsibility to share your knowledge and inspire the next generation. Pay it forward. I have been fortunate to have been guided by others at critical points in my career. For example, when I was an undergraduate at the University of Florida, I saw Professor Herrick Smith putting up a poster for an exhibition of paintings by Harry Stowers, a recent graduate. I challenged the idea that painting was landscape architecture and Professor Smith replied emphatically, "YES, this IS landscape architecture!" His statement had a profound effect on me; I had an epiphany that landscape architecture is an art form, and since then have dedicated my career to that pursuit.

Cultivate a community of creativity. Initiate a weekly salon, "drink-and-draw", or *plein-air* sketching groups as a means to share your work and connect with others.

(195) Chip Sullivan
→ Berkeley, CA, USA

I am continually grateful to my mentors and teachers who led me onto a path of self-discovery and enlightenment. As we all have stood on the shoulders of our teachers, it is paramount for us to pass the torch and light a path for the next generation. Just as American author Carlos Castaneda's mentor, Don Juan, exclaimed: "For me there is only travelling on paths that have heart, on any path that may have heart... and there I travel looking, looking breathlessly."

Scale Error

The world we inhabit is a space made up of various scales. When you regard the world on a microscopic scale, you lose sight of the whole. Similarly, if you try to capture the whole on a macro scale such as that of the Earth, the sky or the universe, you forget to consider small things. By constantly going back and forth between the small and the large, however, we can avoid losing our sense of scale. Fortunately, there are many things surrounding the spaces that we design – plants, buildings, cityscapes – that help us measure scale. Although it is important to use these as "rulers", so as to grasp the space carefully and understand the appropriate scale, it is also crucial to still keep an eye out for the smallest and for the largest – to find, correct or compensate for the "scale errors" that occur in mutual relations between various objects, so as to conceive new situations and spaces.

196 Eiko Tomura
→ Tokyo, Japan

The Surface of the Moon
Looking at the Moon's scenery, it is extremely difficult to recognise whether a mountain is large or small, close or distant. That is because reference objects like buildings, trees, cars and people are absent. Such a slip in perception is fascinating. The landscape of the Moon is formed of large craters, reaching 2,500 kilometres in width, which in turn are entirely made of extremely small regoliths – superficial deposits, around 50–100 micrometres (μm)[1] in diameter – covering almost the entire surface of the Moon, like a blanket.

1   A unit of length equal to one millionth of a metre.

Blurred Boundaries

Once, while I was looking at a blurry picture, I noticed a tiny crescent Moon. It was the only clue that made me aware of the nature of the image – and a space, ambiguous and elusive at first glance, emerged before my eyes. Boundaries delineate a space, but they are not necessarily physical or fixed; blurring them means going beyond spatial and temporal borders, and seamlessly connecting different objects and phenomena. Through this process, the landscape and all the other elements assume equal value. One small plant may be envisioned as architecture – or, alternatively, furniture may be regarded as a compositional element of the scenery. Every time I contemplate a space, I have a good look for boundaries – and then try to blur them and make them ambiguous. In this way, new spatial possibilities can be investigated. I believe new values are to be found in these very boundaries.

197   Eiko Tomura
→ Tokyo, Japan

Revolution 006, Arctic Ocean, NordKapp, 1990
[…] *a relativised view of […] apparent "absolutes" based upon a sceptical stance toward presumed "truths" led [people] to overturn old beliefs and find newer, more factual truths. The heliocentric model provided a more accurate, rational explanation of celestial motions, thus supplanting earth-bound humanly perceived "sense" by an aerially imagined "sense".*

But can we indeed discover cosmic laws within the human mind?

The relation between the brain and the external world resembles the relation between camera and image. The projected image is always an inverted fiction.
Excerpt from "Revolution", Hiroshi Sugimoto
https://www.sugimotohiroshi.com/new-page-80 (accessed 08.05.2021).

Komorebi

When you walk outside you may experience beautiful moments of light and shadow. This can be like the atmosphere of a room whose curtains softly allow light to "pour" inside: many small fragments of sunlight filtered by tree leaves and plants swaying in the wind – this is *komorebi*. When these fragments are projected onto the ground, *komorebi* results in gentle spaces of light and shade. It is important to analyse such a space and to comprehend it as an environment – not only in its planar and three-dimensional composition but also in its materials, textures, density, moments and seasons. Leaves with different shapes and sizes create a myriad of *komorebi*, which results in a variety of spaces as diverse as the trees above them. The gradation of light and shadow projected onto the ground softly connects spaces to one another. We have to remember that *komorebi* is both a natural phenomenon and one that we can design.

198   Eiko Tomura
→ Tokyo, Japan

A portable *camera obscura* in Athanasius Kircher's "Ars Magna Lucis et Umbra", 1646
Komorebi cast on the ground looks like round spots of light. Tree leaves overlap, and the small gaps between them become pinholes, projecting an upside-down image of the Sun. This optical phenomenon is illustrated in the drawing, where projections of the surrounding scenery appear as reversed and mirrored images inside the *camera obscura*. Similarly, a tree becomes a sort of natural camera, casting many virtual images of the Sun on the ground. During a solar eclipse, the projected *komorebi* looks like bright crescents.

Depiction

Accurate depiction is very important, not only to express
and communicate thoughts but also as a means of deeply
understanding spatial and scenic harmony. In a drawing,
a variety of spaces that are usually three-dimensional
inhabit a two-dimensional plane. Temporality is also represented by the depiction of occurrences taking place in
one specific time frame or in different time frames simultaneously. In this way, inaccuracies not found in real things
are introduced into the drawing – and a new reality appears,
combining the real and the virtual. The more detailed
and meticulous the depiction is, the easier it is for us to
accept the imperfections – and the discrepancies between
real and virtual start to disappear from our minds. Those
flaws may actually become a trigger for the imagination.
This is not only part of the allure of drawings but may also
become an effective and necessary process in order
to understand complex spaces and conceive new ideas.

(199) Eiko Tomura
→ Tokyo, Japan

"Kidai Shoran", 1805

Kidai Shoran ("Excellent View of Our Prosperous Age") is a 43.7-centimetre-tall and 1232.2-centimetre-wide picture scroll, meticulously depicting the Nihonbashi area of Edo[1] in 1805. The hand-scroll format allows for a variety of scenes to develop one after the other along the 764-metre-long cityscape. The viewer is able to grasp the space, the way it is used and its scale. The hand scroll also unfolds as a story because it conveys both motion and the passage of time.

1   The city that became known as Tokyo following the Meiji Restoration in 1868.

Spatial Composition

Plants are one of the elements composing a space – and are of equal value to the others. Their contribution is three-dimensional (space formation), visual (scenery formation) and indirect (environment formation). It is extremely important to understand the way in which even a single small plant exists inside a space, and to create spatial meanings and values through each one. I find that building a three-dimensional model and checking its spatial composition makes it easier to evoke new images and ideas. Images of plants printed on a thin film possess a transient, figurative quality; sometimes, they do not show their true nature at all. However, the green hues seen through many layers of film give us a perception of true depth. Then you look at the arrangement and the overlapping of the leaves, and start noticing subtle differences in the spaces created by the plants. Because you cannot see everything precisely, there is room for imagination.

200 Eiko Tomura
→ Tokyo, Japan

Model for planting design study
By placing each individual plant in a physical model it is possible to understand how they exist in a space. Inside the model plants appear and disappear in three dimensions. This allows me to contemplate ideas from a purer perspective. Natural objects do not have a fixed shape, making the design "inexact" – but that is fine. It may be better to figure out a way to complement this inexactitude instead. The appearance and discovery of new and interesting spaces is often a result of this process.

Design is Fun!

Stop considering your job as a job – see it as an opportunity, and consider your abilities as a designer a gift! Recognise that you get to dream all day, explore, research, perhaps even invent, and then materialise all your efforts as tangible expressions! You have the opportunity to build your wildest dreams! Responsibly, of course. This process is incredibly fulfilling, and it will build your character. Have courage and speak up – don't let others spoil your passion or discourage you, but do be receptive to constructive criticism. Understand that you're not alone in this; there are many others who all want the same thing, just from a slightly different perspective. Don't be distracted! Design is not torture – it is fun! It's *having* fun and *creating* fun! Cultivate a fun work environment because that will enrich you and the ones around you, which will be evident to your clients and the users of your projects.

201

Jerry van Eyck
→ New York, NY, USA

"The wonderful world of !melk"
Design should be fun! Channel the joy of being in a happy place! Be thoughtful, mindful and responsible – then make your design a reflection of pure expression and release!

Keep a Cool Head!

Always stay rational. Bold ideas can only live when backed up with research and development. "Working hard" is not the same as "work-related stress". The creative process is fraught with high emotions, frustrations and setbacks, but it is crucial to understand that circumstances are often beyond your control. Learn when to identify this, and become comfortable in your ability to adapt. Know when to say "no"; not every opportunity is worth the effort. Manage your expectations and the flow of your team. Make sure everyone is looked after, and that their view-points are expressed. Tension can build up if members of your team feel unheard – so be the guide who provides perspective and insight. Just as important: stop glorifying all-nighters. You'll gain nothing from them, and they're not cool at all. Manage your time well and be efficient. The art of anticipation can keep a complex project running smoothly and your design resources properly allocated. Don't be arrogant, and ditch the ego – no one is infallible and it's always a team effort.

202

Jerry van Eyck
→ New York, NY, USA

Construction details by !melk/Charles Bronson
as Arthur Bishop in *The Mechanic*
Charles Bronson (1921–2003) kept a cool head during
his entire Hollywood career. He was, and still is, the
coolest of them all. In every role he played, his character was hyper-focused; made decisions based on
accurate information; was efficient, undistracted and
extremely precise. Your management style matters.
Objectivity and rationality will always reign supreme.

Put Your Health First!

Rest well – deadlines happen; however, a burnout is unacceptable to yourself and your team. Exercise – get those 10,000 steps in and take those stairs! Lift some weights if you can. When you feel good, you look good! And when you are content, you are focused. Sleep well – try to get at least eight hours of sleep per night. Make room for downtime to pursue personal hobbies and activities. Eat real and nutritious foods, and avoid processed grab-and-go meals or snacks. Your body is a temple and it's directly connected to your performance at the office. Set an example for your team and promote healthy lifestyle habits. No more sugar! Instead, get your Omega 3, your magnesium, your D3 and B12! Healthy gut, healthy head – which means staying alert and sharp-minded at all times! Push yourself OUT of your comfort zone once in a while! And for the real troopers out there: shower cold!

203

Jerry van Eyck
→ New York, NY, USA

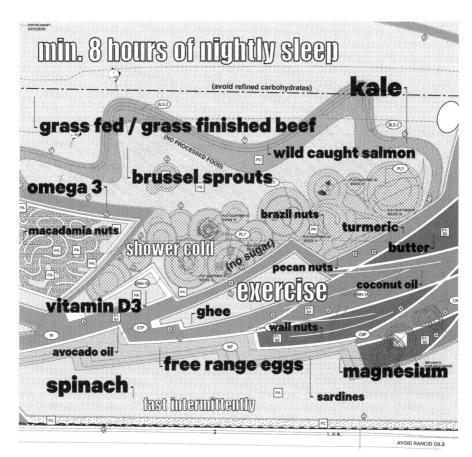

min. 8 hours of nightly sleep

(avoid refined carbohydrates)

kale

grass fed / grass finished beef

(NO PROCESSED FOOD)

wild caught salmon

omega 3

brussel sprouts

brazil nuts

turmeric

macadamia nuts

butter

shower cold

(no sugar)

pecan nuts

coconut oil

exercise

vitamin D3

ghee

ghee

wall nuts

avocado oil

free range eggs

magnesium

spinach

sardines

fast intermittently

AVOID RANCID OILS

Quality designs don't create themselves; they require a designer's clear and focused mind. Consider your personal health as part of the design process. You will be amazed how much your performance and ability will improve when living a healthy lifestyle.

Find Your (Own) Groove!

Don't follow others. Who cares what they do? You didn't become a designer to follow the herd, did you? Think! Communicate! Open your mind and your…skills will follow! Practise, learn, practise again, make a few mistakes, accept your failures and use them as tools of learning and personal growth. Practise more – experiment when there is room for that, and become even better by taking an occasional risk; there is no status quo! Constantly keep educating yourself; your passions, interests and inclinations have real value, and you must develop those traits into tools and new skills. If you can improve a situation, do it! Develop your "voice" and communication style by determining what works well for you and how that can be a unique asset to a project or design team. Push yourself, which leads to pushing boundaries. Don't be afraid to find your own groove! Feel it – and be it!

204   Jerry van Eyck
→ New York, NY, USA

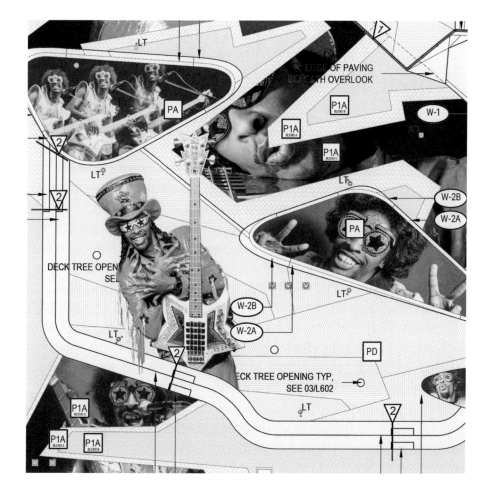

Landscape plan by !melk/Bootsy Collins collage
Bootsy Collins (b. 1951) is the grandmaster of *groove*.
He played with James Brown – and after that with Parliament-Funkadelic, Bootsy's Rubber Band and many others. As a bass guitar player, he developed his own recognisable, unique musical style. There is no one like

Bootsy. https://www.youtube.com/watch?v=IHE6hZU 72A4

Just be you. Find your group or create your own path, but always be unique in your pursuits and define your own path.

Mr Scott Was a Miracle Worker; You Can be Too!

The chief engineer of *Star Trek's* Starship *Enterprise* always invented his way out of complex situations – and you can do the same by inventing brilliant solutions to complex problems, or by anticipating and planning for problems that require multiple contingencies. Nothing is inevitable, there is always a way out – which usually means taking a step back first before leaping forward. Remember, you will never practise design in isolation; there will always be variables (e.g. clients, consultant team members, the economy) that can derail even the most well-managed design project. Never accept unsubstantiated assertions and never settle for less than what you think is actually achievable. Press ahead, and put up a fight if needed. Be clever, learn to think on your feet and draw from past experience. Know when it is appropriate to challenge beliefs or the process, and have your evidence handy! Brilliant ideas thrive when they are demonstrable. And remember: always underpromise and overdeliver!

205 | Jerry van Eyck
→ New York, NY, USA

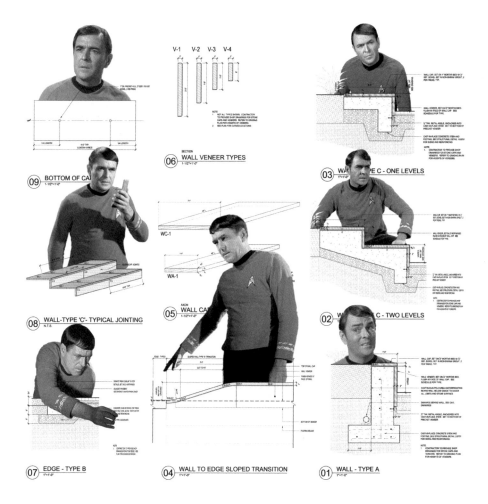

Landscape details by !melk / Mr Scott collage
Chief Engineer Montgomery Scott consistently invented solutions to save the (original) Starship *Enterprise* and its crew from many a predicament. Mr Scott best exemplifies the fact that you don't have to be the captain of the ship in order to have a big impact.
https://www.youtube.com/watch?v=t9SVhg6ZENw (accessed 08.05.2021).

The (Hi)story
of a Landscape

When designing open spaces, real experiences with the
landscape are immensely important. The field trip – i.e.
exposing oneself to the landscape over a longer period
than merely a site visit, and perceiving it consciously
or unconsciously – is, therefore, an ideal way for landscape
architects to acquire these experiences. Sometimes such
a field trip can and may be completely unintentional and
without preparation. It is not directly about the acquisi-
tion of knowledge but about the actual landscape experience. The images of a subjective experience stored in
the memory might only flow into a design years later.
Another type of field trip is directly linked to a design. This
type aims to acquire specific data about a project and
to "read the landscape" by incorporating existing knowledge. Both image-based and knowledge-based design
are valuable techniques that help to read the history of the
landscape and crystallise the issues relevant to the design process.

Günther Vogt
→ Zurich, Switzerland

VOGT field trip, The Netherlands 2014

The Second Law of Thermodynamics

Every landscape architect should be familiar with the second law of thermodynamics. How do the processes governed by it proceed? Are breaks reversible or irreversible? Do they lead to entropy? Even if the general opinion is that physics is a rather insignificant factor in dealing with the landscape, a basic background knowledge of the field is no less important than that of botany, geology or sociology – equally, it enables a better understanding of the landscape and adds a new level to it when designing, which goes beyond the visual–aesthetic dimension.

207 Günther Vogt
→ Zurich, Switzerland

Model test of physical interventions

Profound Knowledge of Botany, Geology and Sociology

Without an in-depth knowledge of botany, geology or even sociology it is hardly possible for a landscape architect to design. From this broad spectrum of disciplinary sources criteria have developed that help practitioners to design landscapes in all their fascinating complexity and diversity. These completely different disciplines naturally presuppose an incredible amount of knowledge, but they are all closely connected to the landscape and appear again and again in one form or another in the process of landscape-architectural design. This specialist knowledge can be enriched and stored – for example, through one's library and a reflective approach – but it can also flow into a design through the design process via a diversely structured team with a wide variety of focal points of knowledge and with intensive dialogue between specialists from the relevant disciplines.

208 Günther Vogt
→ Zurich, Switzerland

Venice Biennale 2021, Venice, Italy
The installation "Migrating Landscapes" addresses
questions about new kinds of ecosystems and globally
shifting landscapes due to globalisation.

The Personal Library – Embrace the Knowledge of Books

One of the most important tools in landscape architecture is the personal library. Every landscape design is closely linked to various disciplines and issues. Regardless of the approach chosen for the design, sooner or later one will come across certain questions that can be answered using a book from one or more of these disciplines. The history of landscape, in particular, can ultimately only be opened up with the help of what has already been written down. Of course, the personal library also has an incredibly strong symbolic value. A landscape architect can quasi-physically embrace the accumulated knowledge of generations in their collection. At a time when, figuratively speaking, even the furthest corner of the world has been opened up, books may actually provide the last chance to experience real adventures.

209 Günther Vogt
→ Zurich, Switzerland

Part of Günther Vogt's personal library

You Never Design for Yourself, but for the People – the Majority of Users Should Agree with Your Design

As landscape architects we design public spaces not for ourselves but almost exclusively for other people. Even if such a person belongs to a group of future users of the realised design, he or she is only a single element of it. The design of a landscape or urban space should be such that the greatest possible number of future users are likely to approve of it. Even if, in a manner analogous to democratic procedures, unrestricted consent corresponds to an ideal value, a "Common Ground" always presupposes a "Common Sense" – i.e. a democratic agreement on what public space means to us in the first place. We should therefore design public spaces not as sole authors but in groups. In this way, the most diverse experiences possible flow into the discussion during the development of ideas, and thus an intersubjectivity – which, ultimately, benefits the design – is already activated in the early stages of development. The increasing privatisation of public space drives this factor further, and makes this issue one that will continue to occupy and influence us greatly in the future.

210

Günther Vogt
→ Zurich, Switzerland

People gather on the steps of the Europahafen in
Bremen on the occasion of a public event.

Landscape Porosity

By 2050, rising sea levels could affect triple the number of people previously predicted – erasing some of the world's great coastal cities, including Bangkok. Southeast Asia, the region with the longest coastline, is at extreme risk. Rooted in agrarian, water-based societies, our cities have now transformed into paralysed concrete developments.

"Landscape porosity" can be understood in this context as a city's capacity to adapt to the natural flow of water, focusing on fluidity and flexibility as essential mechanisms of climate adaptability – especially in the context of muddy, delta cities. The need to shift away from concentrated land-based development is apparent.

Breathable voids and healthy "pore" structures, allowing for the flow and penetration of water and wind, are key necessities. My mission is to defend these ecological spaces through urban context. Bangkok and many other water-based cities serve as an excellent example of how building eco-centric green and blue infrastructures can revive our cities' urban ecosystems.

211 Kotchakorn Voraakhom
→ Bangkok, Thailand

Chulalongkorn Centenary Park, Bangkok, Thailand
For the first time in 30 years of rapid development, an enormously valuable property in central Bangkok was not turned into yet another commercial block. Instead it became a public park that epitomises green infrastructure. Designed for beauty and active use, it also mitigates urban flooding and responds to regional climate change. It includes wetlands, detention lawns, a retention pond and a green roof. Bold concepts contrast with small, intimate moments, reminding us that landscape architecture can help a threatened city learn to live with water rather than fear it.

Reclaim Our Roots

Sitting on the floodplains of the Chao Phraya River, Bangkok is often referred to as the "City of Three Waters". Its trio of hydro-ecological characteristics are formed by the rivers, the rain and the sea. This terrain proves essential to life and its culture, which is deeply interwoven with the natural cycles of water.

This land influenced how we used to live with water. Integrating new design technology and our traditional amphibious living is key. Understanding traditional water management is pivotal to designing effective climate solutions for our changing climate landscape.

Deeply rooted in us, traditional agriculture is the perfect integration of human design with nature. We can interpret our past wisdom to come up with a future-resilient design. For developing countries, imported technology means expensive and high-maintenance equipment. We have often mimicked these without understanding our own cultural maintenance and our changing landscape. Adopting seemingly great technology is not necessarily relevant to our land.

Kotchakorn Voraakhom
→ Bangkok, Thailand

Thammasat Urban Farm Rooftop, Bangkok, Thailand Repurposing 22,000 square metres of wasted rooftop space, the landscape architect helped Thammasat University envision and implement a climate solution with Asia's largest organic rooftop farm – Thammasat Urban Rooftop Farm (TURF). Inspired by the ingenuity of traditional agricultural practices on mountainous terrains across Southeast Asia, TURF creates an inclusive, circular economy for the campus – incorporating sustainable food production, renewable energy, organic waste, water management and public space for all.

On Board at Par

In my country, landscape architecture practices are often perceived in the shadow of architecture. Truth is, we are not simply designers of visual greening aesthetics, we are the creators and fixers of urban ecology. With current environmental degradation, we can see ourselves immersed in that scope of work – and need to combine our approaches in order to figure out climate solutions.

Landscape architecture should not be the last amenity in finishing a project, or relegated to using up the final chunk of the budget for some minor greening. Landscape architecture should be considered as the source of a project's initial concept, as the voice and restorer of a healthy urban environment. If architects and engineers work more collaboratively with landscape architects, I'm certain we can strengthen our climate-focused architecture in very significant ways.

To start a project, we need to get everyone on board at par, to openly discuss and brainstorm – especially across various disciplines – without fear of judgement or domination.

213   Kotchakorn Voraakhom
→ Bangkok, Thailand

Chao Phraya Sky Park, Bangkok, Thailand

In 2020, amid the COVID pandemic, the Bangkok Metropolitan Administration, under Bangkok Governor Aswin Kwanmuang, opened the Chao Phraya Sky Park: the first river-bridge park in any capital worldwide. It represents a collaboration between all professions at par under Chula Unisearch, Chulalongkorn University – and, especially, the voices of the surrounding communities. Forty-year abandoned infrastructure has been given new life as a Bangkok landmark. This project shows that all vacant urban spaces can be reborn as vibrant places – particularly important for the adaptation climate solutions of walkable cities and adding, wherever possible, to much needed public green space.

Compassion *Now*

If you want to be a true professional, you will do something outside yourself, something to repair tears in your community, something to make life a little better for people less fortunate than you. [1] Justice Ruth Bader Ginsburg

I am making landscape architecture as the way to making meaningful life. We dwell in a society that focuses so heavily on individual passion. However, what the world needs most at this moment – from all of us – are acts of compassion, the passion that involves others, as we confront this climate uncertainty. There will be millions of lives devastated, displaced and homeless. Women and children, especially, will always be the most vulnerable in this crisis.

In both practice and education, our generation needs to transmit this generous passion, the compassion, to the young generations of built designers in every way we can by showing them in action. Compassion Now! True professionalism is what we all need to demonstrate.

Kotchakorn Voraakhom
→ Bangkok, Thailand

Lat Phrao Canal Community, Bangkok, Thailand
Porous City Network went into the Lat Phrao community in order to listen to its climate-vulnerable community's needs, and has integrated these needs into their community designs – so different from traditional infrastructure projects in Bangkok. Through a human-centred approach, the landscape architects showed that by working with the community to inform flood-resilient designs, running educational events and raising public awareness of environmental issues, the Lat Phrao community can be empowered with a voice and can live safely by the canal in an age of increasing floods.

1   https://news.stanford.edu/2017/02/06/ supreme-court-associate-justice-ginsburg-talks- meaningful-life/ (accessed 08.05.2021).

Waterscape Urbanism as the Way Forward

In order to address diminishing landscape porosity, every square metre is needed to reclaim resilience so that the land can live with water rather than fear it. Porous landscape innovations can provide a much-needed answer.

However, how many porous parks do we need to sustain a city and prevent it from flooding?

The answer lies not in the number of parks but in permanently returning to our natural waterscape. This is not an option – it is the only way to survive.

An understanding of our adaptive living with water approach is evident in the indigenous processes that are crucial to the waterscape urbanism needed for the future of cities on delta land. To keep our water-based home afloat, we must start by revitalising our canals, floodplains and once porous lands in order to align them with our development as we move forward.

Urban development is inevitable, and the population is bound to grow, while climate change remains an urgent and enigmatic puzzle to solve. But we must consider every possible solution and sign of hope for our future.

215 Kotchakorn Voraakhom
→ Bangkok, Thailand

Chulalongkorn Centenary Park, Bangkok, Thailand
By harnessing gravity, the park can sustainably collect, treat and hold water to reduce flood risks in its surrounding areas. Sitting on a 3° slope, it is equipped with several ecological features: green roof, wetlands, detention lawns and retention pond – leaving not a single drop of rain wasted. The runoff is channelled down through the park's topography to generate a complete water-circulation system. Due to rainfall intensity, and the frequently overwhelmed public drainage system, the park is able to hold up to 1 million gallon (3.8 million litres) of water during heavy rainfall.

Reimagine the Past for the Present

History has a profound role to play in shaping our present and future realms. A critical engagement between the historic and the contemporary in spatial planning and design is an important subject of discourse. With imaginative and sensitive designs, historic precincts can become an invaluable part of the imagination of public spaces, as environmental and cultural assets. Due to distinct context, they have a unique potential to address an aesthetic and spatial uniformity that has become a feature of many developments at the present time.

In the words of Mohammad Shaheer, landscape architect, *Historical relevance implies respect for what has gone before, articulated through restraint in what is attempted today. At the same time, it is probably not wise to look at ruins nostalgically or sentimentally, to maintain them as quaint oddities. So, where possible, historical artefacts have to be looked after in the best possible way to ensure their life, and also find a dignified landscape context.*

216 Geeta Wahi Dua
→ New Delhi, India

Sunder Nursery Heritage Park, New Delhi, India
The site, with many historic structures belonging to the 14th century, lies in a larger cultural zone with the World Heritage Site of Humanyun's Tomb and its gardens and Nizamuddin Basti nearby. Used as a plant nursery during British times in the early 20th century, the precinct, with around 150 mature trees, is now a heritage park. Developed as a series of gardens inspired by historical traditions – with an open-air theatre, an artificial lake, a microhabitat zone and a plant nursery, all integrated as sequential experiential spaces – it is now an integral part of the open-space system of the city. Client: Aga Khan Trust for Culture; Landscape architects: Shaheer and Associates, New Delhi

Traditional is the New Modern

The tradition of the design, construction and maintenance of water-harvesting structures has evolved over centuries in different states of India. They are lifelines for the subcontinent's rural settlements, for their agriculture, domestic and other needs. Over time, they have proved to be examples of resilient systems of collection and distribution of water. In the arid and dry western states of Rajasthan and Gujarat, several such water structures, built with imperial patronage in historic times, are cultural sites–shared, managed, maintained and revered by local communities. They hold invaluable lessons for creating ecologically and economically resilient environments, especially for new developments that strive for the conservation of water resources.

Although all the ten directions are open yet many things have been taken care of while making a choice of the site. This is a pasture for the cow; this is a slope, low-lying area where water will come. [...] then its cleanliness and protection are ensured. [...] Varuna, the water-god is being remembered.[1] Anupam Mishra

217   Geeta Wahi Dua
      → New Delhi, India

Anupam Mishra, Aaj bhi khare hain taalab [The Ponds
are Still Relevant], 1993
This book is a compilation of stories about the planning,
construction and management of water-harvesting
structures by various communities and individuals in
the state of Rajasthan. It documents the life and work
of several of them engaged in harvesting and managing such systems. Interspersed with local myths and
religious references about water, the book (translated
into more than 15 Indian languages) is written in an engaging and personal way, making an easy connection
with – among other readers – farmers belonging to different cultures across the country.

1   Mishra, Anupam (1993). *The Ponds are Still
Relevant* [Aaj bhi Khare Taalab], "From Bottom to the
Top". New Delhi: Gandhi Peace Foundation, pp. 12–13.

The Ultimate Journey is That of Return

With the idea of "greening" the land, derelict wastelands are often afforested with fast-growing plants – frequently, exotic species. If the practice continues for decades, the afforested sites may look like stabilised landscapes but in real terms their ecosystem has been disrupted, with transformed soil character, altered surface and subsurface water regimes, and the associated biodiversity. The intrinsic character of such lands is thus lost forever. They become inert sites with no ecological value or benefit. The restoration approach for such sites may strive to simulate and reconstruct the natural landscape with the reintroduction of native plants or regionally appropriate species. Over a period of revival, the native ecology of the sites, which is truest to their nature, is restored. Once again, they become natural habitats to other life forms – local birds, insects, pollinators, bees and fauna – and occupy their place in the micro- and macro-ecological realms.

Geeta Wahi Dua
→ New Delhi, India

Rao Jodha Desert Rock Park, Jodhpur, Rajasthan, India, 2006

The site, a heavily eroded volcanic hill adjoining a historic fort, had a pervasive presence of *Prosopis juliflora*, a fast-growing tree that was introduced around a century ago with the objective of afforesting the area. With time, it became an invasive species. The restoration process started with the eradication of the mature trees from the rocky strata with the help of the local mining community, followed by improving the soil and planting a range of native species of plants that belong to the rocky microregion. The area is now thriving, with more than 150 species of birds and butterflies. Client: Mehrangarh Trust, Jodhpur Consultant: Pradip Krishen, New Delhi

Know Your City

A strong relationship with nature and its processes is the most significant aspect of the "journeys" of Indian cities – of their evolution, development and survival. Other significant aspects include the location of settlements in the context of natural features and cultural sites – rivers, forests and religious precincts; climatically contextual built forms organised in an organic composition; traditional systems of harvesting natural resources; and a strong sense of community. Such cities comprise some of the finest examples of sustainable living, with a diverse set of attitudes towards nature – functional, aesthetic and philosophical. The narrative of their evolution over different periods informs ways of living with nature and the conservation of its systems and processes for the present-day urban discourse. This learning becomes critical when we "retrofit" these cities to accommodate new needs and functions, and plan and design new ones for the growing population.

(219) Geeta Wahi Dua
→ New Delhi, India

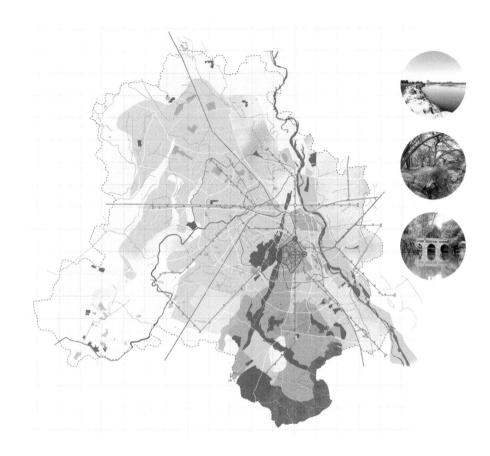

Delhi: Hills, Forest and a River, a study, 2017
This study attempts to examine the changing relationship between nature and the city as seen through the history of the latter. Within its scope, it also identifies and lists the city's important natural and cultural sites. The core idea is to analyse present-day development opportunities and concerns in the light of knowledge of the city's natural and cultural histories in a sensitive and balanced manner. The pilot project was adopted to study other Indian cities, including Pune, Bengaluru, Kolkata and Dehradun. Concept: Geeta Wahi Dua

Embrace the Wilderness

A mosaic of interrelated natural ecosystems encompassing many ecological processes and sub-processes, the wilderness is the true representation of any region's natural ecology. Thriving for decades or even centuries, it marks the natural history of a place, and can form an urban "ecological heritage". It comprises low-maintenance and self-perpetuating landscape, performing important ecological and environmental functions. In spiritual, philosophical and spatial terms, wilderness showcases spaces of serenity and repose, of surprise and wonder, which diverse cultures across the world have celebrated throughout their histories. With more and more parcels of land coming under the ambit of designed landscapes, the wilderness can reveal to designers an enlightened direction in which to imagine landscapes that are ecological, experiential, creative and thought-provoking.

220   Geeta Wahi Dua
→ New Delhi, India

Transgressing Wilderness – Investigating the Wilderness Idea in the Urban Realm, 2020
The book studies the construct of wilderness, decodes it as a mix of complex but discernible spatial arrangements, and links it with elements and variations that lend them their unique character. On the way, it allows us to imagine our spaces in ways that nascent ideas of true wilderness can be introduced so that in time careful stewardship can assist nature to be a designer. Foreword by Aniket Bhagwat; Researcher: Rushika Khanna, LEAF Publications, Ahmedabad.

History as the Basis of Design Art

When I look back over 60 years of practice, certain things stand out as particularly important for design success. One of these is history.

My interest in history began in undergraduate school at UC Berkeley – not in landscape history, as you might expect, but in architectural history. Sitting in a darkened room and drawing from black-and-white slides suggested to me that the significant works of the past were a vast visual resource, one that could be seen in books and visited in person and used in environmental design. The substance of later history courses at the Universities of Illinois and Harvard has stayed with me, while most other coursework has become irrelevant or less valuable over time.

History also taught me to compete not with my peers but with historical greats like Olmsted and Le Nôtre, or the Japanese Zen masters.

221

Peter Walker
→ Berkeley, CA, USA

Barangaroo Reserve has been built on top of a 1950s container port, and is a remembrance of Aboriginal people that lived there before European settlement. It is not a reproduction of previous time – it is naturalistic rather than natural. It utilises sandstone quarried from below the concrete slab and plants not merely from Australia but from Sydney itself. The bluff morphology is built over a great underground meeting hall and an interior parking garage, producing a new raised open space of extended views at the downtown waterside.

Learning to See the Real

The days of the Grand Tour are gone. Today's rich environment of digital and photographic images makes it easy to think you are seeing the real thing. But visiting real sites offers a deeper level of understanding of the basis for design. Adjacent views, temperature, sounds and smells are but a few details in the wealth of information you can gain when you go beyond synthetic images. Stanley White has said that landscape architecture is a cultural enterprise and therefore can be practised as an art – an art of milieu. The creation of that art requires the ability to "see" into complex reality. Over time this gathering of information widens beyond a particular site to include museum exhibits, reading, memories, conversations and, of course, digital and photographic material. But in the beginning much needs to be gleaned from the specific site as a basis for the expression of particular design ideas.

222

Peter Walker
→ Berkeley, CA, USA

The IBM Fountain in Costa Mesa, California, and the "Finite/Infinite" mirrored garden in Beijing demonstrate the complex visual richness possible in characteristics gleaned from observing water elements and simple geometric groves.

Prediction

Given that living materials are central to landscape design, you need the ability to predict spatial effects in projects that are constantly changing over time. These changing states require the designer of landscapes to think in a more complex and fluid way than the designers of more fixed compositions, like those of architecture. I believe this perhaps makes landscape the most difficult and demanding environmental art. From seed to maturity, through seasonal transformation and finally decline, landscape requires the designer to be aware that even the simplest composition is in reality going through continuous slow-motion change. Sometimes dramatic, sometimes subtle, this continuous change requires us to imagine years of successful growth. The simplest composition may in fact become the most powerful over time. The prediction of continued maintenance, or lack thereof, is also important.

223 Peter Walker
→ Berkeley, CA, USA

Before construction began, our National September 11 Memorial design was criticised for being "just a bunch of trees". We responded by commissioning a series of drawings by Chris Grubbs to show the continuing visual interest that a simple grove of swamp white oak produced through a single year (not to mention their growth over a projected 80 years). These drawings solved our problem.

Measuring into Scale

Scale, or apparent size, is both an essential and the most elusive aspect of environmental design. To achieve scale you must be able to measure visited sites and projects with more precision than is possible with photographic images. And when physically present you need a way to quickly and accurately measure what you are seeing.

Happily, a series of simple tools can exactly establish the various heights, widths, lengths and distances in an existing site or garden.

If you know your – and your partner's – height, length of foot and pace, and distance between the extended fingers of the hand, you can measure anything precisely. The height and depth of a bench or a wall, a stair riser and tread, or a tree – can all be discovered, measured and noted. Many of these measurements can be remembered and used over and over again, the humble act of remembering past measurements adding precision to simple observation.

224 Peter Walker
→ Berkeley, CA, USA

The careful measurements and combination of unlike elements such as parking lots, shaded pathways and the architectural combination of windows and beds of ivy have here been composed into a composition of linear elements, both human and monumental, at the Weyerhaeuser Headquarters south of Seattle.

Observation

Landscape programmes are notoriously vague. Rather than depend on a list or some form of functionalist theory, I prefer to find a comfortable place to sit quietly in all weathers and observe how visitors – young and old – walk, stand, sit, climb on a bench or a wall, stop to examine an object, enjoy a view, talk to a companion, or even jump into a pool or fountain. Over time, this simple observation can produce a deeper understanding of visitor use and design potential. Many times, a simple solution may turn out to be more complex and/or rewarding because you understand its range of use. Such design elements as steps, low walls, planned spots of shade or sun, and un-expected views can greatly augment the quality and variety of visitor experience. A conscious script derived from observation may enhance even the simplest phys-ical composition. And you can learn how many mod-est elements serve multiple functions, thereby deepening both the spatial richness and the visitors' enjoyment and even length of stay.

225 Peter Walker
→ Berkeley, CA, USA

Observing a person seeing art in the Nasher Sculpture
Center garden in Dallas, Texas, and a child playing at
the Harvard Fountain in Cambridge, Massachusetts, or
viewing the Alice in Wonderland sculpture in Central
Park, New York are activities rarely included in a land-
scape-design brief. The designer therefore must bring
the depth of programme understanding to a project.

The Art of Looking Down

Whereas architecture has an ambivalent and acrobatic relationship with gravity, the ground is landscape architecture's desideratum. And the fact that there isn't much to see down there is precisely the point. Looking down requires imagination. Looking down is to think of landscape-as-process not picture – ten billion bacteria in every spoonful of soil, no less. Looking down is to try and connect where you stand in the moment with the larger temporal and spatial flows of what Earth Systems scientists (as if they were artists!) now refer to as the "critical zone": the thin bandwidth of life sandwiched between lava and ozone. Looking down is to seek non-Euclidean orientation; to topple the *axis mundi* and Aristotle's *scala naturae* to name but two sacred pillars of urban history. To look down is to turn away from heavenly cities and escapist technological fantasies, and return to Earth to face the fact that the blood of the 6th extinction is on our hands.

226

Richard Weller
→ Philadelphia, PA, USA

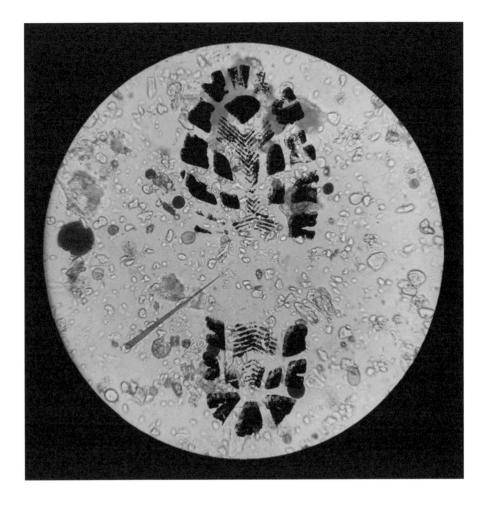

Montage asking what's the *genius loci* of 10 billion
bacteria by Elliot Bullen and Richard Weller.

The Idea
of the Garden

As the primitive hut is to architecture, so the original garden
is to landscape architecture. This garden begins with the
drama of first clearing the forest. Then: fire, meat, stars,
crazy creation stories, dogs, the sowing of seed, livestock,
geometry, and eventually the proverbial hut itself. The hut
multiplies to become a village – then a city, which frames
the garden as a memento of all the city has lost. And now
that the city has engulfed the world, the question is whether
the garden can make a comeback as a viable metaphor
for the world's future – not as a return to paradise but as a
place of labour, care and coevolution. This is a question
of whether this earthly garden will be enough to – once and
for all – settle the human spirit and pull it back from the
brink of its Faustian desires.

227 Richard Weller
→ Philadelphia, PA, USA

The idea of the garden is not a question of either do-
minion or stewardship (originally defined as "Stigward'"
– the keeping of pigs) but a metaphor for the hard
labour and technological precision of ecological reconstruction. Montage based on Laugier's *Primitive Hut*
by Elliot Bullen and Richard Weller

Hard Labour

It's easy to draw a line but not so easy to build one, particularly if that line is retaining earth – which, in the case of landscape architecture, it most often is. To learn respect for lines and the people who build them, every landscape architect should personally build a retaining wall. This crash course in gravity and hard labour should then be extended to gardening and working on farms, where one learns about plants, time, and details that can't be drawn. It is also in gardens and on farms that one meets the unsung heroes of history – the slaves, the peasants and the migrants. The experience of working in the dirt teaches respect for materials, for workers, as well as a restrained use of lines.

Richard Weller
→ Philadelphia, PA, USA

Note to self: remember someone has to build every line I draw; not only that lines can join and link but more often than not they divide, cut and exclude. Montage based on Hogarth's *Line of beauty* by Elliot Bullen and Richard Weller.

The Real Transect

New (old) urbanists like to simplify and categorise cities according to a transect subdivided into six sections with high-density architecture (culture) at one end and low-density landscape (nature) at the other. For them, design should then conform to certain codes related to each of the sections. To challenge this *reductio ad absurdum* and get closer to the raw beauty (and brutality) of the city's psychogeography, I recommend packing some survival gear and trying to walk said transect. But here's the rub: try to stick to one line through an entire city from centre to periphery *without* using streets except when absolutely necessary. Depending on your physical ability, mental resilience and propensity for risk, a stubborn city could take more than a few days, perhaps weeks, to get through, so pack as if for an extreme wilderness expedition – which, in fact, it is.

Richard Weller
→ Philadelphia, PA, USA

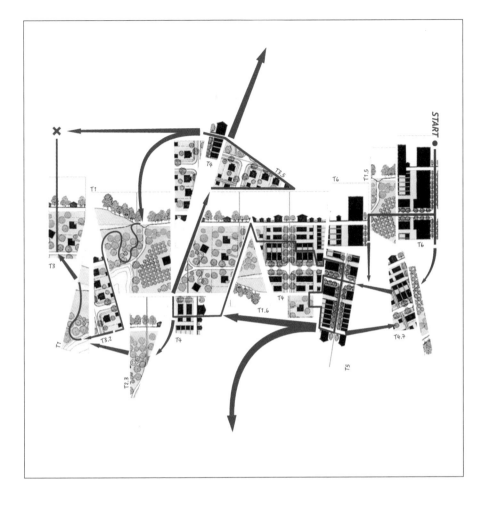

A highly unlikely recording of an intoxicated situationist
trying to walk the new urbanist transect. Montage by
Elliot Bullen and Richard Weller.

Winning and Losing

One of the great highs in a career is winning your first design competition. In a sea of doubt it is a moment of pure, intoxicating validation coming directly from a panel of eminent and most excellent judges. Not only is the win addictive, in many countries entering competitions is an essential way of getting work – which is to say that one also has to get used to losing them. I've said many times that no one ever really loses competitions because everyone gains intellectual property, and it's more or less true. But losing a big one – one you were shortlisted for and then put your heart and soul (and your wallet) into – can be devastating. In this moment of profound invalidation, you shake your fist at the sky, mope in bars and seriously contemplate giving it all away. But above all, you blame the judges – obviously, now a bunch of corrupt morons. As time goes on and you go through this a few times you learn to manage it, but only just. As renowned landscape architect Laurie Olin said to me, the real competition is with yourself.

230 Richard Weller
     → Philadelphia, PA, USA

WINNER

LOSER

Win, lose. A lesson all the same. Montage by Elliot
Bullen and Richard Weller.

"The Untutored Eye"

Imagine an eye ... which does not respond to the name of everything but must know each object encountered ... through an adventure of perception. How many colors are there in a field of grass to the crawling baby unaware of "Green"?[1] Stan Brackhage

Avant-garde filmmaker Stan Brackhage, along with philosophers over millennia, encouraged surrendering what we "know" in order to perceive what we really "see". Artist Robert Irwin says, "seeing is forgetting the name of the thing one sees".[2] And Cy Twombly painted with no spatial hierarchy; our eyes repeatedly flow over the painted surface of his works, creating a new reading with each encounter. Privileging sensory experience over interpretation offers the landscape architect ever-new inputs for visions of each site's potential. In spatial terms this engages us in space and place with participative perception, making a place our own. The mandate for reading a site, therefore, is that of unknowing, direct physical experience.

231 Robin Winogrond
→ Zurich, Switzerland

If you listen to Beethoven it's always the same.
But if you listen to traffic, it's always different.
John Cage[3]

Studies for the winning entry:
Sound Barrier Wall, Grünau. Zurich, Switzerland
The design reframes negative connotations of traffic
and sound-barrier walls, searching for a new poetics
of urban infrastructure. In a kilometre-long glass wall,
varied etched-glass panels gather, abstract, juxtapose
and estrange ephemeral images of daily happenings.
Blurred imagery of natural and artificial light, traffic, natural features, buildings and people in motion contribute
their changing rhythms of time and use. Landscape architects: Studio Vulkan with Robin Winogrond

1   Stan Brackhage quoted in Wees, William C. (1992).
*Light Moving in Time: Studies in the Visual Aesthetics of
Avant-Garde Film*. Berkeley, CA and London: University
of California Press, p. 55.

2   Robert Irwin quoted in Weschler, Lawrence and
Getty Foundation (2008). *Seeing Is Forgetting the
Name of the Thing One Sees: Over Thirty Years of Con-
versations with Robert Irwin*. Expanded ed. Berkeley,
CA: University of California Press.

3   Cage, John (1961). http://www.futureacoustic.
com/silence/ (accessed 08.05.2021).

Geographical Re-enchantment: In Search of the Oddity of Place

Unruly places have the power to disrupt our expectations, of stimulating and reshaping our geographical imagination, to re-enchant geography… Aristotle said "place should take precedence over all other things, it orders the world". Space sounds modern in a way that place doesn't. The reaction of modern societies has been to straighten and rationalize… the oddity of place.[1] Alastair Bonnett

In an unprecedented process of banalisation of our built environment, generic, sterile, urban and cultural land-scapes are replacing distinct, luring and rich places of experience. By contrast, urbanist Susanne Hauser speaks of cities as once places of the unknown, wild, the unexpected, of all things fluid. Alongside the complex demands for projects with ecological and social justice, our profession is charged with building environments capable of offering new, unexpected readings and experience of place with its inherent frictions, contradictions and complexities. Re-enchantment, not to be mistaken with nostalgia, moves us. It's inherently rooted in places able to captivate the imagination, taking us beyond that which we already know.

(232) Robin Winogrond
→ Zurich, Switzerland

Gradually and silently the charm comes over us, we know not exactly where or how. [2]
Frederick Law Olmsted

Landscape is increasingly regarded as a resource serving many interest groups, each with its own voice except one – the landscape itself. Landscape fragments, particularly urban-peripheral ones, are rapidly transforming into well-functioning yet sterile places, unnatural, constructed landscape imagery and semi-natural nature. Contradiction, paradox and friction should become an integral part of contemporary landscape design, nature, atmosphere and sense of place, begging innovative design languages able to express oddity of place.

1   Bonnett, Alastair (2014). *Unruly Places: Lost Spaces, Secret Cities, and Other Inscrutable Geographies.* Boston: Houghton Mifflin Harcourt, pp. xii-xiii, xvi, 251.

2   Olmsted, Frederick Law (1850) quoted in *The Hartford Courant.* Connecticut: The Hartford Courant (2003).

"Nature without an Audience"

At times when terms such as "nature" or "landscape" defy clear definition, not that either of them is waiting around for us to provide one, the expression "nature without an audience" by British writer Jay Griffiths[1] reminds us of her autonomy: nature isn't asking to be perceived. It's our willingness to surrender to our own direct experience of natural phenomena, regardless of how small, that allows us access to their archaic depths. This resonates with what writer Gary Snyder refers to as the green man in us, spoken to when we experience nature in its uncontrolled form — even in a piece of moss. For landscape architects, the intensity of direct experience, as opposed to gathering sources for our designs via the perceptions of others, allows us to express it so strongly in our own works as to affect the dweller in an equally potent way. When we think in terms of natural phenomena, and not natural objects, they can become great sources of power for landscape projects.

233

Robin Winogrond
→ Zurich, Switzerland

Wildwood Plaza, Uster, Switzerland
Writer John Fowles fears a growing emotional and
intellectual detachment from nature. He reveres the
woods for what he calls their "explorability" and "un-
capturability". In the circular clearings of Wildwood Plaza
the dweller can surrender, within seconds, to the pleasure of disorientation that the woods affords us. With no
front, no back, no left, no right, we are left to a state of
drifting. Landscape architect: Robin Winogrond

1   Jay Griffiths quoted in Fowles, John (2010).
The Tree. New York: Ecco.

How We Think City: Recalibrating the Natural

If at first the idea is not absurd, then there is no hope for it.[1] Albert Einstein

Urban biodiversity is one of this century's critical challenges. While we cheer on each new ecological measure, the real need is to radically rethink the premises upon which we build our cities. To date, decisive motors of city planning have been defined by immediate human need. However, we know that drastic change is required at lightning speed and at a large scale. One example of this, "Butterfly Highway", is a conceptual yet realistic proposal to replace 10% of city streets with open soil – allowing for an ecological unfolding within a wide variety of typologies for an extensive array of living matter, reducing temperatures and promoting the water cycle. With millions of organisms living in the upper 50 centimetres of each square metre of open ground, a fine network woven within the urban fabric will reshape our cities as a dialogue between natural and human dynamics.

(234) Robin Winogrond
→ Zurich, Switzerland

"Butterfly Highway", Zurich, Switzerland
In the "Butterfly Highway" concept 10% of city streets
are replaced with open soil for the unfolding of ecology
in living matter. Well-conceived, the benefits are many.
Cities can respond flexibly to the dynamics of natural
phenomena, offer sorely needed space for new forms
of slow mobility and disperse open space throughout
their extent with equality. They can incorporate often-
bulldozed, site-specific morphologies of our urban
environment and experience in a way that asphalt
streets cannot, and encourage new forms of local social engagement in the building of the urban fabric.
Landscape architect: Robin Winogrond

1   https://www.goodreads.com/quotes/110518-
if-at-first-the-idea-is-not-absurd-then-there
(accessed 08.05.2021).

Where Atmosphere and Imagination Linger

The dualism between the external and the internal world had preoccupied philosophers for millennia. [...] For a scientist such as Humboldt who was trying to understand nature, this was the most important question. Humans were like citizens of two worlds, occupying both ... [1]
Andrea Wulf

In our built contemporary landscapes, nature increasingly needs the design mandate of a strong voice to serve as a catalyst of atmosphere and imagination. The potential for natural phenomena to do this lingers in the realm of the in-between, the dialogue between our inner and outer worlds. It demands practical skills to draw it out and create poetic experience. To help "read" the more ephemeral facets of landscapes I created "The Landscape of Three Layers": on the bottom, archetypal natural phenomena, uncontrolled, raw; above that, cultural landscapes of socio-political manifestations on the land; atop both, the "Landscape of Imagination", of memory, longing, desire, experience. When designs activate this last-named layer, works offer "open-ended stories", left incomplete as catalysts for our imaginations, inviting multiple interpretations. To create powerful places the irrational and the intuitive are our strongest tools, combining rational and sensory worlds into intelligence at lightning speed.

235   Robin Winogrond
→ Zurich, Switzerland

One should always be drunk ... But with what? With wine, poetry or virtue, as you choose. But get drunk.[2]
Charles Baudelaire

Sky Platform, Zurich Airport Park, Switzerland
The park consists of a glacier moraine that has been continually transformed over time by large-scale infrastructural projects. In the new park, on still days, the 30-metre-diameter Sky Platform on the summit engulfs the dweller in fog, allowing the sensation of getting lost in the middle of the most connected infrastructural hub in Switzerland. Landscape architects: Studio Vulkan with Robin Winogrond

1   Wulf, Andrea (2015). *The Invention of Nature*. London: John Murray, p. 35.

2   Charles Baudelaire in Louis Simpson (ed. and trans.) (1997). *Modern Poets of France: A Bilingual Anthology*. Story Line Press, Inc. Reprinted by permission of the author and Story Line Press, Inc.

Resist the Urge to do Too Much

Transforming a landscape and leaving one's personal mark on the earth has always been an alluring prospect for all humans – particularly for landscape architects, who are expected to make their names (and fortune) in exactly this fashion. But all too often, so much energy and labour go into reshaping the land that the result is like a new face after plastic surgery: superficially beautiful, but without character or soul. Minimal intervention means approaching the natural landscape as a canvas on which the artist adds only a few deft strokes, and trusts nature to do its own work. To be sure, less intervention usually means greater challenges: the "messiness" of nature often runs counter to popular tastes (to say nothing of the client's vision). Wild landscapes can sometimes look weedy, and harbour snakes – along with bugs and beasts of all kinds. But these are, of course, exactly the things that make a landscape truly alive.

236

Kongjian Yu
→ Beijing, China

The Red Ribbon Park in Qinhuangdao City, China, 2007
Minimal intervention: using a single red bench to transform a former suburban riparian corridor into a popular urban park that serves the ever-growing population of the city of Qinhuangdao. Because no earth-moving work was carried out, not a single tree was cut and no flood walls were built, the impact on natural processes was minimised while fulfilling local residents' needs for recreation and relaxation. Landscape architects: Kongjian Yu/Turenscape

Reopen the Land to the Rain and Floods

Reopening the land to the rain and floods is a nature-based way to retain rainwater at source, slow the often destructive surge of water downstream and be adaptive. The idea is completely contrary to conventional engineering approaches that rely on dams, concrete flood walls and massive amounts of energy used to pump water away from where it naturally flows. Creating "spongier" land not only means protecting and restoring wetlands, which are extremely productive habitats and highly effective carbon-sequestration landscapes, but also creating terraces on steep slopes to stop soil and water erosion, building ponds to catch and remediate fertiliser and pesticide runoff from farmland, creating low dykes along waterways to slow down the flow, and making urban pavements more permeable. Using simple techniques such as cut-and-fill, the landscape can be made spongier in order to retain and remediate water locally, create diverse habitats and make the whole landscape lush and climate-resilient.

237 Kongjian Yu
→ Beijing, China

Sanya City, Sponge City Initiative, China, 2016
Reopening the land to the rain and floods: inspired
by the ancient wisdom of farming and water management – including techniques such as terracing, pond-
ing, dyking and islanding – the formerly flood-plagued
urban centre of Sanya City on China's Hainan Island
was transformed into a water-resilient "sponge city".

Managing water by simple cut-and-fill is arguably the
most effective nature-based solution for adapting to
climate change. Thousands of years of aquaculture in
the monsoon-prone region has helped build a rich body
of wisdom to inspire us in addressing climate change
today. Landscape architects: Kongjian Yu/Turenscape

Create Deep Form

Landscape architecture has become focused on the creation of form. But the form we end up creating is often superficial and fragile, and, as John Lyle put it, "lacks the solidity of coherent process beneath the surface". By contrast, a deep or authentic form "is shaped by the interactions of inner ecological process and human vision".[1] Such a deep form has a sustainable beauty. No interaction between human vision and nature's inner ecological processes is as strong as that between peasants and their land. But this deep connection has been largely broken by modernisation and urbanisation. It is therefore fundamentally important to understand how peasants, with their traditional farming practices and survival wisdom in adapting to a changing environment, transformed their local landscapes to sustain themselves in the face of natural challenges and thereby evolved a variety of inspiring deep forms. In this sense, landscape architecture can be considered as an art of survival that creates deep forms.

238

Kongjian Yu
→ Beijing, China

Sanya Mangrove Park, Ecological Restoration
Initiative, Sanya City, China, 2018
Deep form through designed ecologies: designed ecotones in the form of interlocking fingers help draw
in ocean tides while reducing destructive freshwater
flushes and tropical storm surges. In this case, deep
form helps encourage the natural process of mangrove
restoration and the establishment of a resilient coastal habitat that is rich with species. An area of lifeless
landfill within a concrete flood wall was successfully
restored into a lush mangrove park where nature and
people, ocean tides and freshwater all come together.
Landscape architects: Kongjian Yu/Turenscape

1   Lyle, John T. (1991). (1991). "Can Floating
Seeds Make Deep Forms?" Landscape Journal, 10(1),
pp. 39–40.

Edges Matter

In any landscape, what matters most is the edges – whether between land and water, forest and open field, urban and rural, or built and green space, to name only the most obvious examples. Not only do important energy, material, information and species fluxes occur at the ecotones between any two ecosystems or two types of landscapes, but we humans are ourselves an edge species that evolved at the boundary between savanna and forest – and therefore are particularly sensitive to the landscape edge. Yet at the same time, edges are usually most vulnerable in the built environment: the peri-urban areas are usually the most ignored and chaotic; the riparian edges, which otherwise would be occupied by a diverse set of species, are covered with concrete flood walls; the edges of green spaces have become dumping grounds; and the edges outside buildings are paved with cement. If a project's budget is tight, make sure to invest as much as possible at the edge!

239 Kongjian Yu
→ Beijing, China

Haikou Meishe River, Haikou City, China, 2019
Transforming a grey edge into green: the landscape
architect led the implementation of nature-based solutions to transform a grey, concrete-jacketed river into a
resilient green infrastructure that revives the river with
clean water, rich wildlife, lush beauty and social vitality. The concrete flood walls have been removed and
replaced with eco-friendly and flood-resilient waterways, native habitats have been rehabilitated, wetlands have been built along the river to catch and
clean contaminated runoff, and recreational facilities
have been integrated into the ecological infrastructure.
Landscape architects: Kongjian Yu/Turenscape

Think Like a King and Act Like a Peasant

According to legend, the first king in China was Yu the
Great: a master of water management and flood control,
as well as of fulfilling a vision of peace and abundance
for his subjects. Yet no matter how powerful, a king's vision
can only be realised through the action of each of his
subjects. So it was that one simple tool, a hoe in the hands
of a peasant, which subsequently transformed much of
the territory of China: the terraces that made rice cultivation possible on steep hillsides, the expanses of ponds
and dykes that transformed vast river-delta marshes into
the most productive and sustainable paradises. A wise
king and a peasant have at least one thing in common:
each wants to pass his or her own piece of land, no matter how large or small – and in which they have invested
so much toil – on to the next generation. This ethic is
probably the essence of the profession of landscape
architecture.

240   Kongjian Yu
       → Beijing, China

Yuanyang County, Yunnan Province, China, 2010
A peasant and his land: with tools no more advanced than a hoe, and generations of continuous hard work, hillsides across China have been transformed into a productive and beautiful landscape composed of millions of rice paddies. This same kind of tool trans- formed much of the world's surface long before the advent of industrial earth-moving equipment. It is a profound testimony to how a big vision of a sustainable planet can be realised through techniques as simple as cut-and-fill, using tools as basic as a hoe.

That "Landscape" is Not a Thing

"Landscape" is not a thing. There is no discrete, physical feature of the natural environment one can point to and call a "landscape". Rather, landscape is a social construct. It is the human compositional frame upon the Earth that we project onto it, reflective of our comprehension of the world we live in. As J.B. Jackson writes, landscape is "a man-made system of spaces superimposed on the face of the land, functioning and evolving not according to natural laws but to serve a community".[1] Our values, as a society, are recorded in the landscape; our role then, as landscape architects, is that of scribe.

241 Sara Zewde
→ New York, NY, USA

Wheat fields in Virginia, USA

1   Jackson, John Brinckerhoff (1984). *Discovering the Vernacular Landscape*. New Haven: Yale University Press, p. 8.

"Where the Burial Grounds from the Time of Adam Are"

This is an old Arabic saying, reminding us to be cognisant of our place in history. The entire Earth's surface is a burial ground, an unbounded palimpsest of multiple histories. As landscape architects intervening on that surface, we are asked to intervene in the burial grounds of many past lifetimes – as well as future ones. As such, landscape architecture is inherently in dialogue with generations before and after us. This same Earth will become the grounds for our own imminent burials. Approaching what we do in this regard prompts us to work with care, respect and delicacy, in view of those before us as well as those to come after us.

242

Sara Zewde
→ New York, NY, USA

The Bethel Burying Ground in Philadelphia, Pennsyl-
vania, USA; competition submission by Studio Zewde

The Poetics of a Construction Detail

Big ideas don't stop at the early phases of a landscape-architecture project. Rather, the details of landscape construction – the material expression of the landscape itself – are ripe for the infusion of innovation, idiosyncrasy and poetics. Every corner, every joint, every material finish in the built environment is foundational to the resonance of a landscape with its people, its place and its ecology.

243 Sara Zewde
→ New York, NY, USA

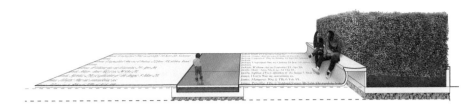

Section profile of the Bethel Burying Ground;
competition by Studio Zewde

That Landscape Architecture is an Inherently Political Act

Land itself is a means of production and a demonstration of power. To design a landscape is to project a vision for how a place ought to be. Some designs seek to reify the way things are; others are projections of change. Either way, designs themselves are campaigns for one or the other, and landscape architecture is an inherently political act.

(244) Sara Zewde
→ New York, NY, USA

Community installation of Africatown Plaza, Seattle,
WA, USA – a project by Studio Zewde for the Africatown Community Land Trust

That Frederick Law Olmsted Wrote a Book about Slavery

In 1852 the *New York Daily Times* (now *New York Times*) commissioned the founder of this profession, Frederick Law Olmsted Sr, to conduct an immersive research journey through the Southern slave states. The country was headed towards civil war, and the paper sought to dispatch the young Olmsted for his ability to reveal the cultural and environmental qualities of landscape in a narrative voice. Notably, Olmsted's period of writing and reflecting on the South would coincide with his work designing and overseeing construction of Central Park, the seminal project of the US profession. In this way Olmsted's reflections on race and slavery in the United States propelled him towards the practice of landscape architecture – and are, in fact, present at the origin story of the discipline.

245 Sara Zewde
→ New York, NY, USA

New-York Daily Times.

VOL. II.....NO. 462.   NEW-YORK, WEDNESDAY, FEBRUARY 16, 1853.   PRICE TWO CENTS.

The first appearance of Frederick Law Olmsted's writing
on the South in the *New York Daily Times*

Verb

Design narratives have been increasingly linked to story-telling, in which nouns and adjectives have been rebranded to form new meanings and ideas such as these ASLA Award-winning schemes: "the Big U" (2016), "Deep Form of Designed Nature" (2020), "Proving Grounds" (2017), "Heritage Flume" (2019) and "Abstracting Morphology" (2017).

These narratives provide big pictures of the visions underpinning projects, which have strong branding ideas behind them. However, the actual design actions/methods are obscured by these narratives. For young designers who are searching for a clearer design vocabulary, there is an alternative narrative approach in which the verb plays the main role. The verbs provide more accurate and vivid design descriptions of the projects, and help build more critical design thinking and analysis.

246 Huicheng Zhong (Atelier Scale)
→ Shenzhen, China

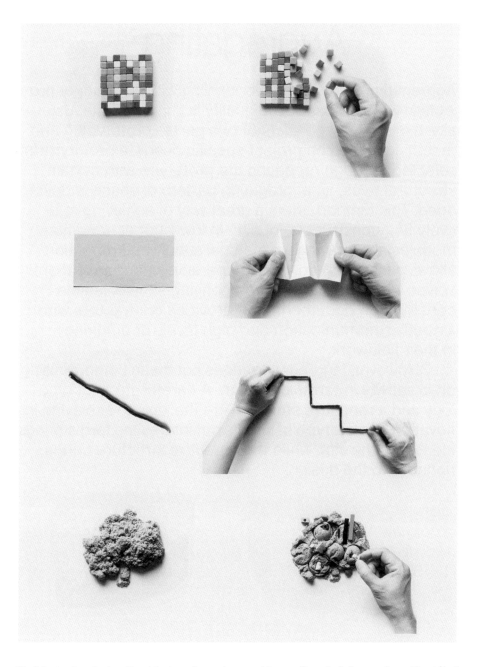

The following four short sections introduces four verbs, each of which addresses one specific design challenge, e.g. "aggregating" – craftsmanship, "landforming" – social space, "terracing" – topography and "furnishing" – lifestyle.

Aggregating

"Aggregating" is a strategy for dealing with low-budget projects in which construction quality is unpredictable. Usually, this strategy consists of two parts – prototyping and repeating. Based on project-specific needs, a prototype is selected; through repeating the prototype with certain structural rules, an aggregating pattern of space is developed. This method offers a great way of achieving relatively fine construction quality in low-budget conditions: modules allow savings in material supply and repetition allows easier workflow, once operatives familiarise themselves with it. And the accompanying simple, legible construction documentation provides contractors with smooth communication and high levels of efficiency in their fieldwork.

However, "aggregating" does not mean compromising on creativity in terms of design. A careful study of typology and a repetitive structure are the keys to achieving innovation. A prototype of simple but interesting forms brings identity to the site, while the repetitive structure brings richness to the design.

(247) Huicheng Zhong
→ Shenzhen, China

The Wave, Shenzhen, China, 2020
The Wave was a low-budget and recyclable display garden at the 2020 Flower Show in Shenzhen. The landscape architect devised a prefabricated modular system, through which the garden could be rebuilt on another site with 90% of its material reused after the flower show was over. The module prototype was inspired by the texture of the ocean, which forms a backdrop to the city of Shenzhen. Through the tilting and moving of modules (repetition), a field of waves is created to simulate the ocean. Landscape architects: Atelier Scale

Landforming

"Landforming" is a design operation that aims to create social space. Landform not only brings powerful sculptural qualities and aesthetics to design but also accommodates a range of programmes in modern landscape architectural works. In the West, influenced by Modernism, landscape architects have emphasised the performance of landform in their design. Examples include Byxbee Park, Palo Alto, California, by Hargreaves Associates (ecological treatment), Cumberland Park, Nashville, Tennessee, by Hargreaves Jones (community programmes), and Storm King Wavefield, Mountainville, New York, by Maya Lin (sculptural park).

In traditional Chinese gardens, by contrast, landform has been used to emphasise experience. The design process was triggered by how people experienced the space, and many design decisions were made on site. The emphasis on bodily movement in landforming provides a dynamic perspective on place making. We could learn from both of these types of wisdom on landforming.

248　Huicheng Zhong
→ Shenzhen, China

The Folds, Changzhou, China, 2020
The Folds is a community playground that mobilises children's perceptions of landform. It is designed with the notion of returning to basics through the folding of spaces, and the use of playground equipment is deliberately minimised. The spatial sequence starts from a folding lawn and transitions to similarly contoured wooden decks. This distinctive landform encourages children to perceive the space with their hands and feet. They can run, climb, play hide-and-seek and decide how to have fun by themselves. Landscape architects: Atelier Scale

Terracing

"Terracing" is a site-specific strategy responding to topography. It can be understood as the creation of programmed rooms on sloped/graded sites, and its simplest applications can be studied through sections.

Once a site with changes in elevation is cut into terraces, it requires negotiation between the horizontals and verticals. The wider the flat space, the taller the accompanying vertical façade will need to be – while the shorter the vertical façade, the narrower the horizontal space is. Behind this logic lies a series of considerations of comfort, habitability and views. Therefore, a careful study of proportions based on the varying site challenges is needed.

(249) Huicheng Zhong
→ Shenzhen, China

Restroom in the Mountains, Yantai, China, 2019
Restroom in the Mountains is a functioning public toilet as well as a terraced courtyard constructed on existing topography. The courtyard is threaded through with a series of transitions between toilet blocks and landscape pavilions. The setting of the viewing deck provided a waiting place and the best viewpoint of the nearby mountains. A dialogue can be observed between the horizontal "landing", created for programmed spaces, and the layered vertical façades. Architect and landscape architect: Atelier Scale

Furnishing

"Furnishing" is an important design consideration in addressing how people enjoy their daily lives. In a highly developed industrial society, instead of specifying customised furniture, it's tempting for landscape architects to choose outdoor furnishings from product lists for their works – which is a cost-effective choice. However, an outdoor furniture set is not a simple aesthetic and economic consideration; there are other, social and cultural, factors involved. Designers should always pay more attention than they are inclined to do for furniture design, which accommodates most of human social behaviour. And there are many smart strategies we could use for furniture settings; here are some tips:

First, "site impromptu" – furniture design can be integrated with site features such as grade change.

Second, "modular design" – modules can bring rich combinations and interactions to the sitting environment.

Third, "surprise" – it doesn't need to look like furniture; have people discover and explore the way they want.

250 Huicheng Zhong
→ Shenzhen, China

Raindrop Garden, Shenzhen, China, 2020
Raindrop Garden is a commercial rooftop garden that is open to the public. It accommodates a wide range of furniture – for example, a wooden-capped low retaining wall, seen welcoming a visitor to rest and take off their shoes (top left); a super-wide benchtop with storage space beneath, offering a mini-playground for toddlers (upper right); a raised "*tatami*" wooden deck, providing an area for casual chats (middle right); and movable chairs for bar-type seating on wooden decks (bottom). Landscape architects: Atelier Scale

Illustration Credits

About the Editor

Cannon Ivers is a chartered member of the Landscape Institute and a Director at LDA Design in London. He holds a Master of Landscape Architecture degree with distinction from the Harvard University Graduate School of Design. Cannon is a teaching fellow at the Bartlett School of Landscape Architecture, London and the author of the book *Staging Urban Landscapes: The Activation and Curation of Flexible Public Spaces* published by Birkhäuser. His professional work includes the design of urban parks and public spaces, and he frequently contributes to design discourses through publications examining 3D design and digital fabrication; spatial programmability; intelligent water design; and high-impact, low-maintenance planting design.

Layout, cover design
and typesetting:
Lisa Petersen,
Bureau Est, Leipzig / Paris

Editorial supervision
and project management:
Henriette Mueller-Stahl,
Berlin

Copy editing:
Ian McDonald, Solva

Production:
Heike Strempel, Berlin

Lithography:
bildpunkt Druckvorstufen GmbH,
Berlin

Paper:
120 g/m^2 Salzer Touch white

Printing:
Eberl & Koesel GmbH & Co. KG,
Altusried

Library of Congress
Control Number:
2021940525

Bibliographic information published
by the German National Library
The German National Library lists
this publication in the Deutsche
Nationalbibliografie; detailed bibliographic data are available on the
Internet at http://dnb.dnb.de.

ISBN 978-3-0356-2335-2
e-ISBN (PDF) 978-3-0356-2336-9

© 2021 Birkhäuser Verlag
GmbH, Basel
P.O. Box 44, 4009 Basel,
Switzerland
Part of Walter de Gruyter GmbH,
Berlin/Boston

9 8 7 6 5 4 3 2 1

www.birkhauser.com